Punch Debt in the Face,
Invest for the Future,
and Retire Early!

KICKING FINANCIAL ASS

PAUL CHRISTOPHER DUMONT, MBA, CFA

Paperback ISBN: 978-1-9991326-0-6
E-book ISBN: 978-1-9991326-1-3

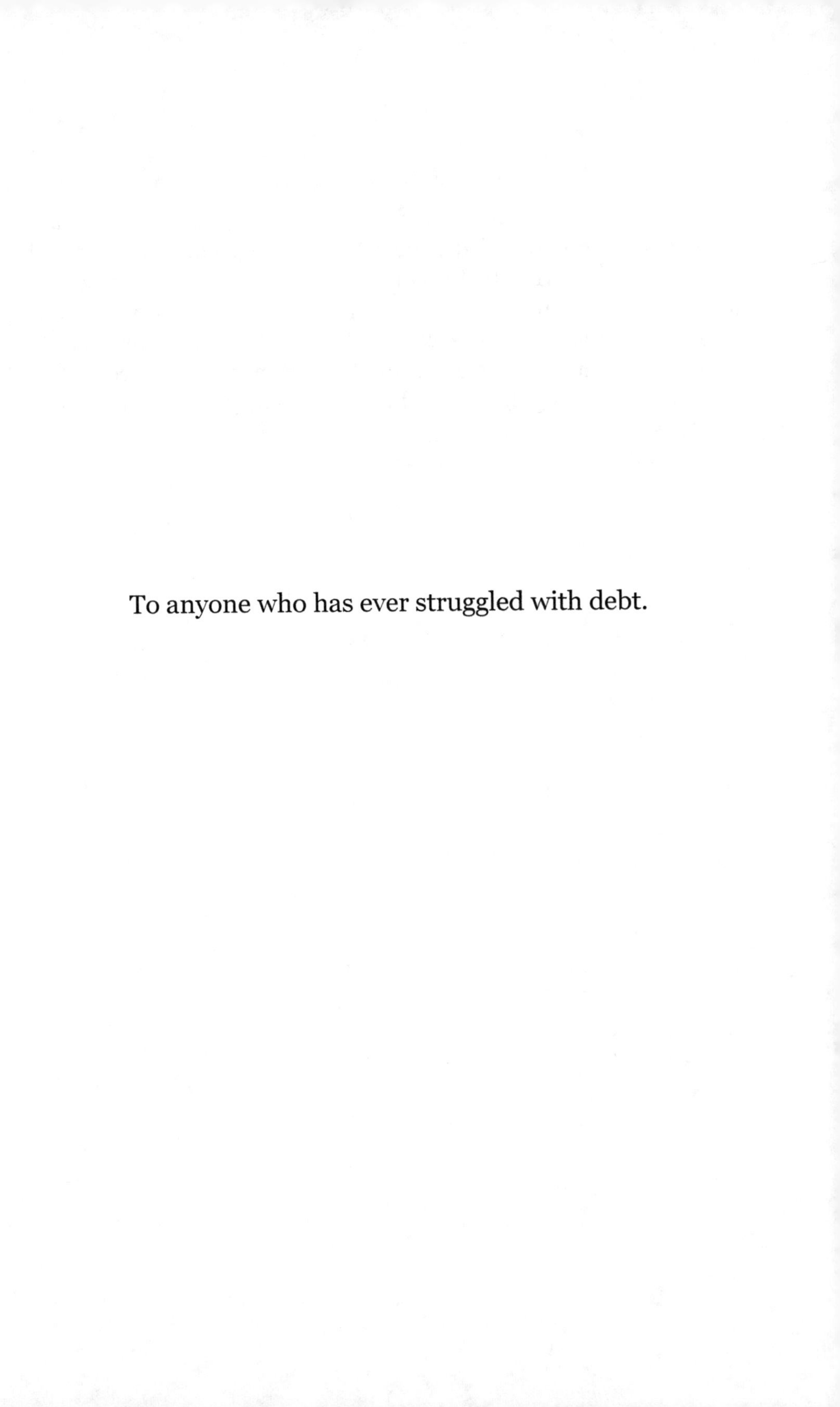

To anyone who has ever struggled with debt.

CONTENTS

NOTE FROM THE AUTHOR

I wrote *Kicking Financial Ass* because I, like many Millennials, struggled with the challenges that our generation faces, including enormous student debt, lack of economic opportunity, and competitiveness in the job market. While searching for answers to questions like, "Why do we spend money?" and "What do I need to know to be financially secure?" I determined that there was a not a single book on the market addressing my concerns. Years after my debt was paid off and had bought my first property, friends and family started asking me for financial advice. After seeing success after success, I decided to share my experience with others.

Most books fail to address how our values toward money influence our buying decisions. We chase happiness by trying to buy our way there. Furthermore, most books do not definitively answer the key questions: How much money do you *need* to retire? Why use retirement accounts? Should you buy or lease a car? Is real estate a good investment? This book tackles those questions by condensing a wide breadth of material into simple concepts you can apply in your daily life.

This work rests heavily on the shoulders of countless other books, blogs, studies, and articles written about financial affairs and the contributions of individuals acknowledged at the end of the book. Moreover, I have been interested in personal finance for over 15 years, investing in the stock market since I was 18, and have applied all I learned from my finance undergraduate degree, M.B.A., and CFA charter. From this research and experience, I consolidated the best financial advice into an easy-to-read "how to" guide on retiring earlier and living your life to the fullest. As a side note, I work 9 to 5 like most of my readers, but I am on track to retire in 10 years even though I had $50,000 of debt only four years ago.

WHY SHOULD YOU READ THIS BOOK?

This book is not a boring lecture on money but rather a roadmap and tool you can use for your situation. It does not need to be read in order, so start at the beginning and continue to the end or flip to the chapter you feel will be most beneficial. Each chapter has actionable advice you can apply immediately to improve your finances.

You will come away with strategies to help you save, even if you are barely scraping by today. You will receive clear advice on paying down your debts—credit cards, student loans, or mortgages. I provide transportation advice on whether you should buy a new or used car, lease, or use ride sharing. You will discover the differences between 401(k) and IRA accounts for Americans and RRSPs and TFSAs for Canadians. I also discuss tricky situations such as negotiating salaries and raises. You will learn what to invest in and whether it is better to rent or buy a home. You will also learn the most crucial lesson of investing: Start early and why that matters. But most importantly, you will learn how to retire in as few as 10 years.

Take your time when reading this book and reread sections when necessary. For example, focus on Chapter 8: Negotiate Salaries & Raises when you start looking for a new job to maximize your income. I discuss financial concepts and stats throughout the book but in a way that anyone can understand. After reading this book, you will be much more confident with your finances instead of being overwhelmed when trying to balance a budget.

While some of the examples are extreme, they illustrate how saving even $10 a day allows you to retire years earlier. This book is not about being a hermit, saving every dollar you possibly can, and eating Kraft Dinner every night in hopes of a better future. It is about maximizing life's fun at minimal expense by using a simple, effective investment strategy of investing in index funds.

So, whether you choose the sections that most apply to your life or read the entire book, I hope you take away a few ideas that you can use to improve your personal finances and are prepared to retire in as few as 10 years.

Now, it's time for you to start *Kicking Financial Ass!*

— Paul Christopher Dumont, MBA, CFA

INTRODUCTION

Saving money is hard. We want to budget, but we spend more than we realize—or admit to ourselves. For most, money seems to come and go, and we are left wondering why we are in debt. Life gets in the way, and unexpected expenses pop up. At the same time, costs for education, housing, and healthcare tend to increase every year, outpacing the raises we receive. The media does not help either. We turn on the TV and are overwhelmed by the information that is available. We ask ourselves where to even start. Between investment accounts, budgeting, and what to invest in, there is a lot to take in. Not only that, but the media portrays happiness as being for sale, and modern life pressures us into overspending with new cars, new watches, and new iPhones. It is no wonder that it is hard to save. We keep postponing saving money until later, thinking once we get that promotion or raise then we can start.

I used to think this way, especially when I was younger. I remember buying a new MacBook Pro for school and spared no expense getting the 15-inch version with bumped up specs when I only needed the 13-inch base model. I upgraded my iPhone every year when my current iPhone still worked fine. I bought the latest and greatest TVs to keep up with technology. And, I spent countless hours looking at new cars when I could afford them the least. Fortunately, common sense reeled my car fantasies back in. This behavior did not mean that I was a bad person. In fact, most people live life this way.

GROWING UP WITHOUT

As a child, my brother and I grew up with a single mom. Our dad left when we were young, so we did not have a lot. During the day, my mom worked multiple jobs to try and make ends meet. I remember on more than one occasion seeing my mom walk in the door with a box of food, knowing she had gone to the food bank. In school, I was picked on for having odd clothes and glasses because we could not afford what the other kids were wearing. Through it all, I thought that if only I had what the other kids had, then I would be popular, happy, and normal. My urge to impress others came from this. I thought if I worked hard and bought everything my mom could not afford, then I could impress others in school, be liked, and have more friends.

Why am I sharing such a personal story right off the bat? Because coming from nothing, I know how hard it is to get your life on track and how it is easy to feel frustrated, exhausted, scared, resentful, or guilty over your financial situation. My experience growing up also taught me that happiness is a state of mind and how the insecure boy wanting to keep up with everyone else to be happy was wrong. **I only became happier when I was satisfied with what I had.**

Growing up without money meant that I had an odd fixation on it. I did not have money to manage, and, therefore, I wanted it. For years, I dreamed of what it would be like to have money and believed that once obtained then I would finally be secure in myself and have something to offer others. This became a problem because my self-identity revolved around money and how insecure I felt not having it. Little did I realize that money should be the process of attaining more but not the end goal.

My life changing-moment came after graduating high school, when I decided to live with my dad for a year in the Philippines. While I was there, I saw little children with literally nothing, whose parents made less than $100 a month, running around in the streets laughing. I thought to myself, "How can they be happy? Here I am working hard at my job at McDonalds spending money on videogames and electronics, and these kids are happier than I am." I needed to change my focus, so I studied how those children could be happier than most people I knew back in Canada, including myself. No longer was I trying to impress others. Relationships, volunteering, and making a difference in the world became my focus. The good news is that you can make those fundamental changes right now like I did.

WHO IS THIS BOOK FOR?

I wrote this book to make a positive impact on others concerning financial security. It is written to teach a new way of thinking about money—to help readers learn the fundamental skills they need to become debt-free and retire comfortably. This book is for anyone, of any age and income, who wants to learn how to better save their money and change their mentality regarding their finances. The ideas in this book are not taught in the classroom, although they should be, and come from real-world experience. I have an undergrad in finance and an MBA and still had to learn everything from scratch.

I specifically wrote this book as a guide for my peers, Millennials. We tend to focus on experiences instead of financial security, mostly because we believe having both is not feasible. We may wonder why even try when faced with seemingly insurmountable odds. The principles of this book, however, teach everyone the monetary fundamentals and demonstrate how financial security is achievable no matter where you come from.

TACKLING DEBT

The number one financial issue that faces society is debt. In December 2017, U.S. consumer debt hit \$3.82 trillion. That is a lot of debt. Of this, \$1.75 trillion are student loans, \$1.25 trillion are auto loans, and $500 billion are credit cards. And, this does not include mortgages. Think about that for a second. This debt is about $11,660 per person[1] including children. For a household of four, that is about $46,640. What is even more astonishing is the average U.S. household has a savings rate of 3.2%, which is near a 10-year low. As seen in the figure below, the country is headed in the wrong direction. Canadian consumers are doing a bit better but not by much.

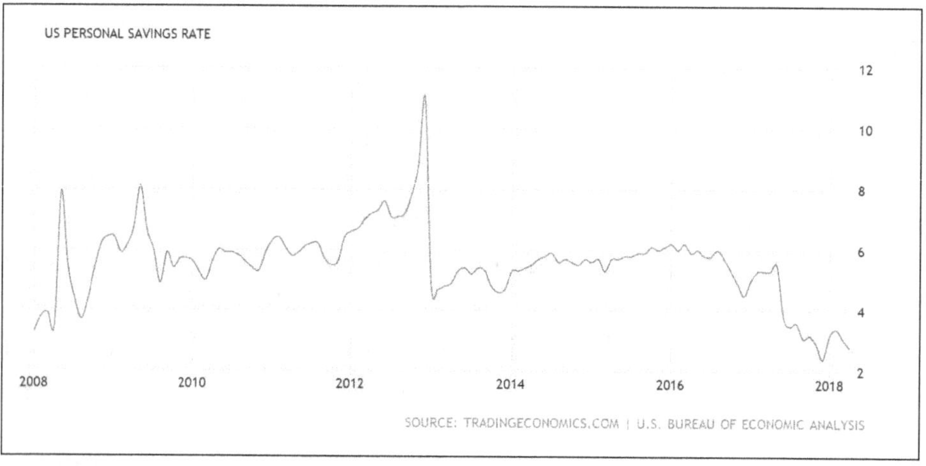

If you are one of the 99% of the people out there, you fall somewhere on this financial spectrum:

1. Retired comfortably with no money issues.
2. Working, saving the maximum in tax-advantaged retirement accounts, and have no debt other than a mortgage.
3. Same as above, but add car loans and/or student loans.
4. Same as above, but not able to max out your tax-advantaged retirement accounts due to expenses.
5. Same as above, but have credit card debt.

6. Living paycheck to paycheck, cannot always make payments on time, and have a troubled credit history.

7. Near bankruptcy, likely to lose the house and personal possessions, cannot find work, and debt is higher than your ability to pay back.

Your goal is to move up this spectrum, one rung at a time. My goal is to help you get climbing!

For full disclosure: I am in the #2 category with my goal of obtaining #1, which is a far cry from where I was growing up. What qualifies me to write a book about personal finance when I am not myself retired? Good question. First off, I started from the bottom with literally nothing. I was not born into a rich family. I had to work and claw my way up out of poverty.

Second, I am now debt-free, and believe me, it felt like a long road from being over $50,000 in debt and making mistakes along the way to now having a sizable six-figure retirement fund and owning multiple properties. It is all about saving, budgeting, investing in the market, using compound interest, and the time it takes for your money to work for you.

The truth is that for most people it is not one single event that puts them into debt but rather hundreds of small financial decisions every day—one transaction at a time, each swipe of the credit card, nothing that sets off alarm bells on its own. These small purchases add up over time, though. While my debt primarily came from a single life decision, I show you how changing my daily spending habits allowed me to pay back my debt and save a sizable amount in a short period of time.

The 14 chapters in *Kicking Financial Ass*, which are divided into four parts—Foundations, Growth, Investing, and Living Your Life—will transform your relationship with money, help you achieve your goals, and enable you to become financially independent. This is not a book about money as much as it is about changing your perspective on life.

BY THE END OF THIS BOOK, YOU WILL:

- ☑ Spend less money and be happier.
- ☑ Save more money.
- ☑ Lower your debt and question every purchase.
- ☑ Focus your time on what matters.
- ☑ Overcome your past money mistakes and start investing for the future.
- ☑ Save for retirement and retire earlier.
- ☑ Discover what values you hold dear.

After reading this book, you will feel empowered to change your habits and routines, focus on debt reduction, and ultimately retire. You will feel free to travel the world, take multiple vacations a year, and live life how you want to and feel secure in your financial future. Many of us never received financial training in school. Most, if not all of us, had to learn it on our own. This book is a short-cut to teach you everything you need to know.

PART ONE

FOUNDATIONS

Now that you are motivated to make changes, which ones should you make to take control of your finances to keep them on track?

This section of the book focuses on the foundations of money management that will teach you the essentials to take control of your finances, walk you step by step on how to rethink your money habits, build your confidence, eliminate your debt, and start saving, allowing you to live your life to its fullest potential. Do this by:

- Being satisfied with what you have and spending money on the things that make you the happiest,

- Knowing how much you need to retire and determining how much you can afford to spend,

- Learning how to budget and be frugal and not cheap,

- Learning strategies on how to tackle your debt in the most efficient way,

- Building a small emergency fund in the shortest time,

- Minimizing your car expense so that you can focus on growing your money,

- Having insurance to protect you from unexpected life events, and

- Learning how to say no to overspending.

These essentials allow you to propel your finances to the next level. So, get ready!

CHAPTER ONE

BE MORE WITH LESS

THE STORY OF THE MEXICAN FISHERMAN

A businessman was sitting at the pier of a tiny coastal Mexican village when a fisherman docks a small boat. The businessman compliments the fisherman on the size of his fish and asks him how much time it took to catch them.

"Not very long," replies the fisherman.

The businessman then asks why the fisherman did not stay out longer and catch more fish?

The fisherman says he has enough to support his family and does not need more fish.

"What do you do with the rest of your time if you're not catching more fish?" the banker asks.

"I sleep late, fish a little, play with my children, take siestas with my wife, and, in the evenings, I go into the village where I drink wine and play guitar with my friends. I have a fulfilling life."

The businessman is not impressed.

"I have an MBA from the top business school in the world and can help you," he says.

"You should catch more fish, and with the profits, buy a bigger boat. With the profits from the bigger boat catching more fish, you could buy more boats and eventually have an entire fleet of boats other fishermen can use to fish for you. Instead of being the middleman, you could sell directly to the fish processor, eventually opening your own processor. You could own and control the entire supply chain, everything from owning the product to the processing and distribution of the fish. Complete vertical integration," he says. "You could then move from this little village to New York City where you would run your growing business."

The fisherman, intrigued, asks, "Seems like a lot of work. How long would that take?"

"If everything goes well, at most 25 years," replies the businessman.

"Then what?" asks the fisherman.

The businessman laughing says, "That's the best part, when the time is right, you sell your business to the public by doing an IPO and make millions!"

"Wow. Millions, I can't even imagine. Then what's after that?"

"After that, you'll be able to retire, live in a tiny village, sleep late, play with your children, catch a few fish, take a siesta with your wife, and spend your evenings drinking and playing guitar with your friends."

The moral of the story is that you can become more with less. The Greek philosopher Epictetus said, "Wealth consists not in having great possessions, but in having few wants."

The fisherman already achieved his end goal, so pursuing wealth for the sake of money was futile and frankly a waste of time. If you are going to pursue money, pursue it for a reason. Money should only be a process in obtaining your goals, not the means in itself. The first thing you should do then is to determine what your reasons are when wanting to make money.

Too often, people get wrapped up in the wanting more, more, more, thinking, "If only I had more money, I'd be happy...," believing, consciously or unconsciously, that the next purchase will be the cure-all to their problems. In the 1943 influential paper, "A Theory of Human Motivation," American psychologist Abraham

Maslow proposed that healthy human beings have a certain number of needs, and that these needs are arranged in a hierarchy, with some, such as physiological and safety needs, being more fundamental than others, like social and esteem needs. Maslow's 'hierarchy of needs' is often presented in a five-level pyramid, with higher needs prioritized only after lower, more fundamental needs are met. Looking at the pyramid, we often are trying to achieve esteem and self-actualization needs by buying our way there.

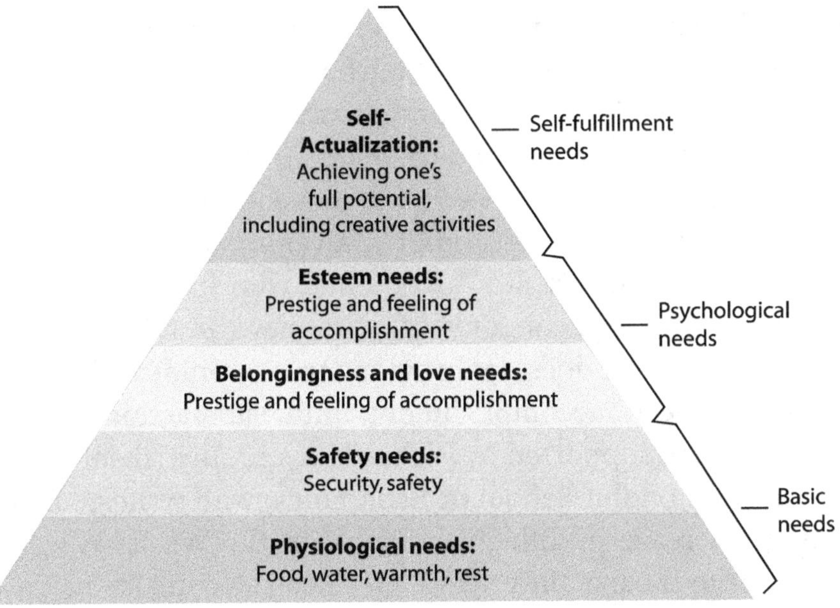

If we apply this model to our financial lives, as long as our basic needs are met, money adds little to our happiness. Ironically, by chasing the next big thing, we tend to jeopardize our safety needs by being less financially secure. As a result, we can feel stressed about finances, insecure about where we are in our careers, and dependent on a certain income. If we go too far, we cannot afford to do the things that really make us happy.

Many people say that money does buy happiness, and they would be right. Statistically speaking, household income is strongly related to both emotional well-being and a person's evaluation of their own quality of life—up to a point. Past that, however, there are diminishing returns between dollars earned and happiness. Multiple studies show[2] that after making $75,000 to $80,000 per year, the difference in the emotional well-being an extra dollar makes in reducing negative emotions becomes less and less. The difference between earning $20,000 and $40,000 is huge and life-changing. The difference between earning $120,000 and $140,000 means your car might have nicer seats. The difference between making $1,000,000 and $1,020,000 is a rounding error. You require a certain amount of financial security before you can move onto your other needs and move up the hierarchy.

After over a decade of studies, University of Illinois psychologist and researcher Dr. Edward Diener, who specializes in what makes people happy, concluded that money can add pleasure to people's lives, but it does not bring the true happiness that comes with self-respect, accomplishment, and satisfaction. Diener's conclusions are supported by Richard Layard, British labor economist at the London School of Economics, who writes, "Despite our huge increase in affluence, people in the West have grown no happier in the past fifty years." We keep striving for more and more things, living in the most prosperous historical period of all time, and yet, we are not getting happier.

"The desire for more positive experiences is itself a negative experience," Mark Manson points out in his book *The Subtle Art of Not Giving a F*ck*. "And, paradoxically, the acceptance of one's negative experience is itself a positive experience."

Manson goes on to say that the more you pursue feeling better, the less satisfied you become, as pursuing something only reinforces the fact you lack it in the first place. The more you desperately want something, the more you feel inferior. It is a nice thought that we can ultimately reach some sort of "ultimate happiness." But alas, this can never be. What made us happy today may not make us happy tomorrow, whether it be buying that new $80,000 car or $500,000 house. We constantly feel inadequate. Psychologists refer to this as the "Hedonic Treadmill."

This predicament goes by many names. Historian Yuval Noah Harari in his book *Sapiens* refers to it as the "luxury trap." He asks, "How many young college students have taken demanding jobs in high-powered firms, vowing that they will work hard to earn money that will enable them to retire and pursue their real interests when they are thirty-five?" He warns, "But by the time they reach that age, they have large mortgages, children to educate, houses in the suburbs that necessitate at least two cars per family, and a sense that life is not worth living without really good wine and expensive holidays abroad." We become used to life's luxuries and are caught up with wanting more, never satisfied.

This is causing some serious social consequences. Economist Arun Abey in his book *How Much is Enough?* says:

"Youth and adult suicide rates have doubled or tripled over the past forty years. The biggest-selling drugs are those treating depression, anxiety and stress. The onset of depression now occurs at age fourteen, anxiety at age eleven. Obesity and diabetes have reached epidemic proportions."

We are trying to chase happiness but never seem to get there. How can we ever be content?

WHAT MAKES US HAPPY?

Most of your assumptions about happiness are likely wrong. Psychologists[3] over the years have found that people are bad at perceiving happiness and estimating what will or will not make them happy. Furthermore, multiple surveys[4] show that despite differences in income, geography, culture, and gender, people tend to have the same level of happiness on average. If these are not reliable predictors of happiness, then what is?

WE ARE BAD AT DETERMINING WHAT MAKES US HAPPY OR UNHAPPY

Most people believe if they won the lottery, they would be much happier. However, on average, when measured a year later, people who had won the lottery were not any happier than those who had not.[5] There have even been accounts of lottery winners taking their own lives because they thought they would be happy, but the money changed their lives negatively, either through changing their relationships with friends and family or feeling like they did not deserve the money.

We are also bad at remembering what made us happy or unhappy in the past. Previous moments are, most of the time, not as unpleasant or enjoyable as we remember them. Our brain generalizes one feeling for an entire event. If we remember a moment as pleasant and enjoyable, we tend to remember the entire experience as pleasant and enjoyable. Equally so if the experience was unenjoyable.

HAPPINESS TENDS TO BE MISCONSTRUED AS PLEASURE

When people want happiness, they tend to seek pleasure, which is not the same thing. Pleasure is related to happiness but is not the cause of happiness. Ask a drug addict how their pursuit of happiness turned out. Ask a recovering gambler, who lost everything, whether the pleasure of gambling made them happy.

Research proves[6] that people who focus their efforts on materialistic pleasures end up more emotionally unstable and unhappy over the years. The seeking of materialistic pleasures often forms the basis of a focus on money. More money can afford more pleasures, yet something rings hollow. There is more to life.

We have all heard of a story from a coworker, friend, or family member who had a lot of money and yet was still miserable. At the same time, we have heard that saying, "Money may not buy happiness, but I'd rather cry in a Jaguar than on a bus." The question then becomes how do we make enough money to meet our basic needs while focusing on our self-fulfillment needs? The goal is to have enough money to have our own version of a Jaguar but not cry along the way. We want to be happy right now, however, money is part of the process of getting to where we want to be and should not be the end goal.

OUR VALUES SHOULD DRIVE WHAT WE DO

True, long-lasting happiness is derived from the deeper values we define for ourselves. Our ultimate happiness is not defined by what we do and what happens to us, but why we do what we do and why it happens to us.

Think about what motivates you. Is it an intrinsic or extrinsic motivation? Being motivated to make money just for money's sake will lead to an unstable emotional state and superficial behavior. Having a deeper purpose like making more money to take care of your family will be more rewarding. Although, it is easier said than done. Most of us compare ourselves to others, trying to keep up with the people we interact with daily and those in our community, both online and in-person. If you compare yourself to someone who makes you feel financially inadequate or broke, change that. How? Focus on your own race, meaning your life.

Everyone comes from different backgrounds and life experiences. It is likely the people you are trying to keep up with are struggling financially, so keep that in mind if you find yourself comparing yourself to others. When we compare ourselves upward, we tend to feel inadequate. There was a study published in 1992 that compared Olympic athlete's reactions after winning either a gold, silver, or bronze medal. The researchers, Victoria Medvec, Scott Madey, and Thomas Gilovich, found that silver medalists were unhappier than bronze medalists. The reason? The silver medalists felt they just missed out on winning gold, while the bronze medalists were happy to receive a medal. The same idea goes with comparing our financial situation to others.

Comparing our financial situation and seeking the approval of others can lead to neediness and be a turn off to those same people. On the other hand, if you are motivated by the approval of your closest friends, then that can help you through good times and bad. For example, I do not let my financial situation define who I am. Who I am is separate from my finances, and I take comfort in knowing my friends love and care for me regardless if I have money or not. Your values dictate your perspective on money. Change your values, and you will change your perspective and allow you to take control of your finances.

Write down what you want written on your gravestone, and then write down what would be written today if you passed away. Albeit a bit morbid, this powerful exercise develops a perspective and vision regarding your values. On your deathbed, the last thing you want is a list full of regrets and people remembering you for the wrong reasons.

The top five regrets of the dying[7] as observed by an Australian nurse who spent years working with patients during the last 12 weeks of their lives are:

1. I wish I had the courage to live a life true to myself, not the life others expected of me.

2. I wish I hadn't worked so much.

3. I wish I'd had the courage to express my feelings.
4. I wish I had stayed in touch with my friends.
5. I wish I had let myself be happier.

Focus on limiting your life's regrets and concentrate on what you feel in your heart. Remember, no one writes on their tombstone how much money they had.

Steve Jobs said it beautifully:

"Remembering that I'll be dead soon is the most important tool I've ever encountered to help me make the big choices in life. Because almost everything— —all external expectations, all pride, all fear of embarrassment or failure— —these things just fall away in the face of death, leaving only what is truly important. Remembering that you are going to die is the best way I know to avoid the trap of thinking you have something to lose. You are already naked. There is no reason not to follow your heart."

THE HAPPINESS EQUATION

One way to think of happiness is as an equation:

$$\text{happiness} =^{8} \text{reality - expectations}$$

Another way to think of it, which is advocated by Neil Pasricha in *The Happiness Equation,* is:

"Want Nothing + Do Anything = Have Everything"

The idea is that you can work on lowering your expectations, improving your reality, or both to be happy.

Reducing happiness to an equation oversimplifies it but can be useful. The largest flaw with this approach is the belief that happiness is derived from being without. In other words, if you decrease your expectations, you still view happiness in terms of external validation. Life is about growing, achieving, failing, and learning from everything in between. It is better than raising your expectations to become happier, as long as you are internally rather than externally motivated. You will be made happier by setting a goal and failing to achieve it than setting no goals in the first place. At the end of the day, many complex factors play a part in what makes us happy.

According to a November 2017 National Geographic study, the three happiest places in the world were Singapore, Denmark, and Costa Rica. What does each of these places have in common? "Their people feel secure, have a sense of purpose and enjoy lives that minimize stress and maximize joy." What is so intriguing about the study's results is that people living in each country do it in differing ways.

- People in **Singapore** are very achievement-based, so they are focused on improving their reality.
- In **Denmark**, the joke is that people living there are happy because they have low expectations.
- The people of **Costa Rica** are somewhere in between.

I found this to be true with my own experiences abroad. When I was 18, I lived in the Philippines for a time and saw people living on less than $10 per day leading happier lives than most people I knew back in Canada. I saw children with literally nothing but a tattered shirt and worn out sandals playing in the street with a smile on their face. I watched people sacrifice what little they had for complete strangers, which brought joy. Close relationships were everything to them, and it did not matter if they had money or not. People in each country focus on different components of the happiness equation to be happy. Which part you focus on determines what you should do in your pursuit of happiness.

CHANGING YOUR EXPECTATIONS

"True happiness is to enjoy the present, without anxious dependence upon the future, not to amuse ourselves with either hopes or fears but to rest satisfied with what we have, which is sufficient, for he that is so wants nothing. The greatest blessings of mankind are within us and within our reach. A wise man is content with his lot, whatever it may be, without wishing for what he has not."

— Seneca

Research published in *The How of Happiness* by University of California psychology professor Sonja Lyubomirsky tells us exactly how much of our happiness is based on our life circumstances. The shocking figure? 10%.

Ten percent of our happiness is what happens to us, and the other 90% is based on our own expectations of the world. Expectations, not material wealth, play the biggest part in being happy.

There are two ways to change our expectations: Rethinking our Perspective and Practicing Gratitude.

1. Rethinking Our Perspective

There are about 7 billion people on Earth today and 115 billion people who have ever lived in the history of the world. That means 108 billion people are dead. Most people have already lived their lives and will never experience the pleasures of life again. They will never experience having kids, watching them grow up, growing old, and enjoying simple experiences like watching the sunset. Being alive means we have won the lottery.

Next time you look up in the sky, look at the stars. Hundreds of billions of them are out there, and this planet we call Earth is the only planet we know that has life. It makes any problems you are experiencing small in comparison to the vastness of space.

Look at median annual incomes across the world, adjusted for purchase power parity (PPP). If you make more than $1,500, you are already better off than more than 50% of the planet.

Do you make more than $50,000 per year? Forget about the top 1% because you are in the top 0.31%. It would take the average laborer in Ghana 312 years to make the same amount. If you are reading this book, chances are you either had the money to buy it or the time to read it. Either way, you are better off than most people in the world.

Next time you have a bad day, take the time to reflect and count how lucky you are.

2. Practicing Gratitude

What do Oprah Winfrey, Richard Branson, and Tim Ferriss have in common? They consciously practice gratitude.[9] Gratitude is defined as the quality of being thankful, a readiness to show and return kindness. Psychologists have said that when we appreciate the present, we become happier. Some studies have shown that being grateful can increase happiness levels by as much as 25%.[10]

Grateful people are more giving, less selfish, and more generous. Gratitude brings people closer together and improves relationships. Ray Dalio, one of the most successful hedge fund managers in the world, said one of the secrets to happiness is having "meaningful relationships." Being grateful toward others helps build these meaningful relationships.

Gratitude is real. To practice gratitude, write down the good things that happen each day. One way to do this is to keep a journal. I use the 5-Minute Journal, which was recommended by Tim Ferriss, but you can use any form. Either before bed or as soon as you wake up, write the top three things you are grateful for and spend a few minutes thinking about them. After a few weeks, look back and reflect on your list of things you were grateful for. It will change your expectations of what really makes you happy.

CHANGING YOUR REALITY

"You will never be happy if you continue to search for what happiness consists of. You will never live if you are looking for the meaning of life."

— Albert Camus, philosopher

What most people do not realize is that happiness does not come from money. One part of the happiness equation stems from changing your reality or, in Mark Manson's words, "solving problems." To be happy, we need something to do. It is an activity, not something that is passively bestowed upon you after the purchase of something. It does not magically appear after you receive that raise or promotion or finally have enough money to buy that new car.

Living day-to-day brings its own set of problems to solve, like what are you going to eat for dinner, planning a date, and so on. Happiness is a work in progress because solving problems or taking action is a work in progress. When you solve your health problem by getting a gym membership, it creates a new problem of working up a sweat, having to shower before you go to work, and changing so that you do not stink up your workspace. There is always more work to do, more happiness to pursue. Note that Manson means that *solving problems* is key, not having problems you are unable to solve.

According to Tim Ferriss in his book, *The 4-Hour Workweek,* the question you should be asking isn't, "What do I want?" or "What are my goals?" but "What would excite me?" "Excitement is the more practical synonym for happiness, and it is precisely what you should chase. It is the cure-all."

What creates excitement? Taking action. Want to take ballet lessons? Do it. Want to learn how to scuba dive? Do it. Want to learn a new language? What is stopping you?

To progress, you need action! Every big name in the world is advocating it. Action, not money, makes you happy. This is how you change your reality with the happiness equation.

> **"You're not supposed to optimize for money; you're supposed to optimize for happiness."**
>
> — Mr. Money Mustache

You should take action to feel more control over your life.

TAKE ACTION TO FEEL CONTROL

Taking action makes us feel like we have control over our lives, which helps drive how happy we are over the long term. People who feel they have little-to-no control experience low levels of happiness, regardless of their circumstances. They can be rich, famous, or have won the lottery, but if they feel they had no control over it, like they did not earn or deserve it, they will be unhappy and likely depressed. This explains why some celebrities become addicts and even take their lives.

How do you take control of your life? There are three ways:

1. **Take responsibility for your actions**. You cannot control everything that happens in your life. Setbacks happen to everyone. The difference is how you respond.

2. **Set goals and achieve them.** No matter how small, setting daily goals builds momentum and allows you to accomplish big things over time. For example, if you

work out for 20 minutes a day, eventually you will find yourself more fit in the mirror.

3. **Minimize your reliance on external validation**. External validation is seeking approval from other people. It is about how you feel you appear in society. Internal validation, on the other hand, raises self-esteem and baseline happiness.

FOCUS YOUR SPENDING

While taking action allows us to feel control over our lives, we still spend money almost every day. This is not to say you should not spend money, but be conscious toward the things you spend money on and ensure that they will improve the quality of your life in the most measurable way. They should be meaningful to you, not to your friends or family. One way to implement this approach when spending money is to ask yourself, "Will this take away a negative?"

Tim Ferriss suggests creating a list of things that drive you crazy or drag down your quality of life. Spend money to solve these problems, and test these changes weekly to find the smallest changes in spending that result in the biggest increase in happiness. For example, I find that having unreliable cell service makes me frustrated. I would rather pay a higher monthly fee from a reliable carrier than pay less with a budget company. The cost to my sanity would be too great if I tried to save money on an inferior service.

Another approach is to write down the things you spend money on regularly that do not bring you happiness. Then, create another list that brings you happiness and rank each on a scale from 1 to 5. By performing this exercise, you identify and remember what expenses make you feel happy or unhappy. So, the next time you swipe your card, you will be able to remember your motive. When you understand what triggers feelings after a purchase, you can reflect and avoid the expenses that make you feel broke, guilty, or afraid and focus on the spending that brings you joy. Over time, cut back or eliminate the expenses that make you feel guilty, like taking an expensive taxi home or buying a house you cannot afford.

LEARN FROM THE BEST

If you want to retire earlier and be happier, learn from the best. What is the recommended way to do this? Mimic people who have done it before. The book *The Millionaire Next Door* studied the habits of the wealthiest people in the world. The authors, Thomas J Stanley and William D Danko, studied the habits of the people they perceived as rich: Those with big homes, fancy cars, and living in wealthy suburbs. They came away surprised. The people they interviewed had high incomes but were drowning in debt. They were spending more than they were saving, running on the "Hedonic Treadmill." Not only that, but they were miserable worrying about their finances. Remind you of anyone you know?

The authors then changed their tactic to look for people who had over a million dollars but lived modestly. What they found was shocking. They discovered that "over 80% of U.S. millionaires are ordinary people who have accumulated their wealth in one generation." People with actual wealth followed the tried-and-true philosophies in this book by living on less. They are long-term investors, own shares, avoid debt, and save. They live in modest homes and neighborhoods. They do not focus on material possessions and are happier.

Remember, peak happiness per dollar is achieved when you make between $75,000 and $80,000 a year. Then why save and invest to have more money? The reason why is so you can retire *faster*, maintain that level of income throughout your retirement, and do things you love in your spare time. The most precious resource in the world is not money but TIME. The only way to gain time is to cut back your spending now so that you can save more, invest more, and be happier now by focusing on things that will actually make you happy like gratitude, meaningful relationships, and taking control of your life.

SUMMARY

Changing your attitude about money has everything to do with investing and budgeting. To be able to live within your means, budget, and save for retirement requires an entirely different perspective on money altogether. While this book serves as a guide for what you need to do to retire, it all starts with your attitude about money.

- Aim to be happier without using money as the influencer. Ask yourself, "What do I need right now to be happy? Do I need anything other than what is happening right now to be happy?" "Am I being externally or internally motivated?" Focus on what makes you happy and your core values.

- Remember the happiness equation: You can work on changing your expectations, improving your reality, or both to be happy.

- To change your expectations, rethink your perspective or practice gratitude. When it comes to rethinking your perspective, focus on how lucky you are. You are alive right now and likely in the top 1% of the world's population in earnings. As for gratitude, remember that it brings people closer together and improves relationships. The world's top performers all recommend it.

- Set goals and achieve them. Taking action allows you to feel like you have control over your life, which leads to greater happiness over the long term.

- Focus your spending on items that not only improve the quality of your life in the most measurable way but are meaningful to you, not to your friends or family.

- Learn from the best. Your next-door neighbor could be a closet millionaire. People who avoid debt, save money, invest wisely, and live in modest homes and neighborhoods are happier on average. These people have realized that happiness is driven by things other than money.

CHAPTER TWO

KNOW WHERE YOUR MONEY IS GOING

FIND OUT YOUR NET WORTH

Most people are not sure where their money goes. After the big expenses, like rent and food, it is like the rest of the money just disappears. It does not help that many have debt. I have been in debt for most of my adult life, between paying for my undergrad and then my MBA. And, let me tell you: Saving and paying down debt does not become easier with time. It seems that something always comes up to take priority.

Most people should not strive to become financial experts, but rather, we should learn enough to make our money work for us.

NO REGRETS: A FRESH SLATE

When it comes to money, it is hard to wonder, "What if?" What if I bought Apple stock when I had the money? What if I bought a house 20 years ago? What if I was better with my finances? Financial regret. This regret can destroy your confidence in your financial future, making it impossible to trust your financial decisions. It eats at you and reminds you of how you arrived at where you are. Trust me. I have a long list of missed opportunities. It is hard to let go of the frustration and resentment. The good news is that you are making the right decisions now and starting with a fresh slate.

To take control of your finances, first make peace with the past. To accomplish this, find out how much money you have earned in your lifetime, and then find out your net worth by creating a balance sheet of assets and liabilities. Having a positive net worth is good because it means you have more money than you owe. The second step is to track expenses. The final step is to create a budget by separating your accounts into buckets. The more you can automate your accounts, the easier it will be to save.

FIND OUT HOW MUCH MONEY YOU HAVE EARNED

How do you know how much money you have earned in your lifetime? A short-cut is to dig up old tax returns and look at your gross income. You can look up bank statements online, too. Knowing this number helps with a few things:

1. You have a better sense of how much money has entered your life and what is possible in the future.
2. It opens your eyes to how much money you have earned.
3. You know where you sit financially today.
4. It will reset your relationship with money.

Find Out Your Net Worth

What do you have to show for all that income? Your net worth is your total assets minus your total liabilities. In other words, the value of everything you own subtracted by the total of everything you owe. For many, this number will be negative, meaning you owe more money than you have. This may or may not be a surprise, but the extent of it might. That is okay because it is better to know.

Net Worth= Assets – Liabilities

On a piece of paper, write down the following, with the dollar amounts, to determine your net worth statement:

Liquid Assets

- Cash
- Savings bonds

- Savings accounts and checking accounts
- Investments—mutual funds, index funds, stocks

Fixed Assets

- House: Use a realtor or an appraiser for an estimate of your house.
- Vehicles: Look up the blue book value.
- Any other material possessions you can put a value on if you think someone would be willing to buy it. Exclude any depreciating consumer stuff like your furniture or consumer electronics unless you are ready to sell them right now.

Liabilities

- All debt, which includes the balance owing on your house, the balance of your car payments, and student loans.
- Any other loans of any kind.

Once you write everything down and complete the equation, you have your net worth. Why have a net worth statement for your finances? You now know where you stand in your financial life and can begin to plan to reduce your liabilities over time. If you do not know where you are financially, you cannot start to improve your financial situation.

Statistics show that those who monitor their budget on a regular basis are more likely to stick with it than those who do not.

To accumulate money, you need to know:

- How much you are spending,
- Your financial net worth, and
- How to invest your savings productively.

There is no way around it. You *need* to understand your spending, and you *must* invest your money, so remove any barriers.

WHAT SHOULD YOUR NET WORTH BE?

The average net worth by age of Americans is broken down like so:[11]

Age Range	Net Worth
Less than 35 years old	$6,900
35 to 44 years old	$45,740
45 to 54 years old	$100,404
55 to 64 years old	$164,498
65 to 69 years old	$193,833
70 to 74 years old	$225,390
75 years old and over	$197,758

For millennials, the median net worth is $6,900. That is scary. The primary reason is student loan debt as people are coming out of university, often with a net worth that is negative until they turn 30. Even still, the average American peaks at a little over $225,000 in net worth in their 70s before it starts to drop as they draw on their savings in retirement. This is not enough to retire! Unless your annual spending rate is $9,000, most people will be continuing to work throughout their later years.

What should your net worth be then to be above average? Rules of thumb, such as dividing your age by 10 and multiplying that number by your annual gross income, exist, but these estimates are flawed. There is no right number. The most important thing, especially in your 20s, is to start building your net worth and pay off your debts. Choose the age you want to retire and work backward. If your goal is to retire by age 40 and you are 25 right now, determine how much you need to save per year to hit the 25 times your annual spending rate.

BUDGETING TECHNIQUES

Budgeting sounds easy enough, but most people do not budget. One of the most widely adopted budgeting tools is the 50/30/20 budgeting plan. The idea is that you spend 50% of your money on necessities, 30% on discretionary items, and 20% on savings. The problem with this approach is having to track every expense. Tracking expenses, creating artificial budgets, and trying to dictate how you should live your life is an idea that just makes me want to give up. And, what constitutes a necessity? At what point are you spending too much on food and clothes? Therefore, I recommend the 60/40, spending/savings budget to start.

In *The Barefoot Investor*, the author, Scott Pape, recommends having three financial buckets where you put your money on autopilot and never think of it again. Those are your blow, mojo, and grow buckets, or in other words, your spending, emergency fund, and savings bank accounts. I agree with this approach. However, I like to add a fourth bucket, your short-term savings bucket. Your buckets or bank accounts would look like this:

Spending bucket:

Daily expenses.

Emergency bucket:

Safety money. Save at least $1,000 at first, and then once you are debt-free, build it up to two months of your salary as an emergency fund.

Savings buckets:

- Short-term: For the occasional splurge, vacations, and down payments.
- Long-term: For your long-term wealth and security.

Using this system, you can pay off your mortgage, create an emergency fund, and save for retirement all at the same time. It is simple, but it works. The goal is to be able to explain to someone in 30 seconds or less how you manage your money. If you cannot do that, your budgeting technique is too complicated and less likely to be successful.

What portion should you put into each bucket? The benchmark should be to spend 60% of your income, i.e., your spending bucket, and to save 40%, also called 60/40 budgeting. That is impossible you say, "How can I live on 60% of my income?" It is easy once you know how to save money. Moreover, if you can dedicate 40% of your income toward index funds, you will be able to retire in 22 years. If saving 40% is too hard, start a side hustle to increase your income. I discuss this in detail in Chapter 9: Have a Side Hustle. You can either decrease your expenses or grow your income to meet the 60/40 budget. Thousands of ways to increase your income exist. Dual incomes help but are certainly not required.

If this is not possible, then adapt. Let's say you are unable to work and are dependent on a set income while supporting a family or are a single parent. It is best to shoot for the moon. If you miss, you will still be among the stars. Meaning, if you find saving 40% of your income is impossible, aim for 30% or even 20%. Common advice is to save 10%. So, if you are saving more than that, you are doing better than most. That said, I still believe hitting the 60/40 ratio is doable for most and should be the goal for all, especially if you follow the advice in this book. Now, let's break down the various buckets.

Emergency Bucket

The emergency bucket is easy. It is saving $1,000 in the beginning. Then, after you are debt-free, save two months of income.

Building up to $1,000 should be your #1 priority. Use any additional savings you have to create the emergency fund.

<u>Spending Bucket</u>

While each expense item is flexible depending on your circumstances, aim to achieve these percentages with your spending bucket:

- Housing (rent or mortgage payments): Spend 25%
- Food: 5% to 10%
- Utilities (power, gas, water, broadband internet, and phones): 5% to 10%
- Transportation: 5% to 10%
- Insurance: 5%
- Miscellaneous: 5%

For example, say you make $60,000 a year or $5,000 a month. After taxes, assume you take home $4,000 a month. This is what it could look like:

- Housing: $1,000 a month
- Food: $400 a month
- Utilities: $250 a month
- Transportation: $250 a month
- Insurance: $200 a month
- Miscellaneous: $200 a month

Total Monthly Expenses= $2,300 or 57.5% of $4,000
Savings= $1,700 or 42.5%

In the miscellaneous category, I included entertainment expenses, and eating and drinking were categorized as food. Use this only as a guide, however. People with lower incomes will spend a higher percentage of their income on housing and food, for example. But what if you are on a variable income, e.g., you work on your own or freelance? In that case, keep your fixed costs as low as possible. This allows you to keep your automatic payments on schedule.

But wait a second, where are debt repayments in that budget? Debt repayment should be your **#1 priority after creating your $1,000 emergency fund!** Every spare dollar you have after creating an emergency fund should go toward paying down your debt. In the above example, if the budgeter had debt and already had an emergency fund, then $1,700 a month should be used to pay that debt down. See Chapter 5: Take Back Control of Your Debt for detailed advice.

As mentioned, this is just a guide, but your ultimate goal should be to get your monthly expenses below 60% of your income. I have no debt, so I have no debt repayments. If you have debt, I recommend living closer to work to save on driving expenses and having a roommate to save on housing costs.

The 40/60 budget is what I aspire to and how I live. I have lived on 40% of my income for over three years, saving 60%, and managing to pay down $50,000 of debt, save up down payments for multiple properties, and have a six-figure retirement portfolio. Going to this extreme, I would be able to retire in 10 years. It is up to you to know what you are comfortable with, but I highly recommend overhauling your entire financial situation to the 40/60 split. This strategy is easier once you hit the first 60/40 target.

Savings Buckets

Once you have an emergency fund and are debt-free, work toward your retirement. If you want to retire in 22 years, save and invest at least 40% of your income in investments. If you want to continue working until you are 65, then spend more than 60% of your monthly income. However, I assume you want to retire sooner than later. Every dollar you invest in your long-term savings bucket should double within 7 to 10 years if you buy stock market indexes. If you are 25 years old, then your money should double five to six times before you turn 65. Learn more about compound interest and index funds in Chapter 10: Invest in the Index.

Tailor the exact amount to *your* retirement goals. Try to save at least 40% of your monthly income by setting up automatic withdrawals into two separate bank accounts. I recommend dividing your savings accounts into short-term and long-term, with automatic withdrawals going from your paycheck checking account into each of the two accounts.

Short-term savings: Short-term savings is for saving up for a down payment on a house or paying for a car or vacation. Splurges also fit into this account. You have some flexibility, but the most I would put into this account is 20% of your income after taxes, preferably less.

Long-term savings: Long-term savings is for retirement. Ideally, set aside most your savings for retirement, i.e., more than 20% of your income, because the more you invest now, the sooner you can retire. If you save 20% of your income in long-term investments, expect to retire in 37 years. If you save 30%, 28 years. And if you save 40%, 22 years. If you save 60%, like me, 10 years.

Often, people forget to invest the money from their long-term savings account. To avoid this, see if your bank or online brokerage can invest the money automatically. If not, then follow these three rules for your long-term savings bucket:

1. If your checking account balance is greater than $1,000, transfer all the money into your investing account.

2. If your investing account balance is greater than $1,000, invest all the money into the index of your choice. See Chapter 10: Invest in the Index.

3.   Never break Rule #1 or Rule #2.

It is too easy to try to time the market if you are not automatically set up to buy the index. So, stop trying to make financial decisions and automate it. The more you can automate this process, the less you will fall victim to the harmful biases investors can have. And to be sensible, automation simply makes your life easier.

Use Dual Incomes to Your Advantage

If you have a spouse or partner who brings in an income, then use the dual incomes in your favor. A proven way to retire in less than 10 years is to save one salary and use the 60/40 budget on the other.

Say your household after-tax income is $100,000, with each spouse making $50,000 a year take home. To achieve the 60/40 budget, save $20,000 from one spouse's salary (saving 40%) and then 100% of the other spouse's income. This equals $70,000 out of a $100,000 combined salary or 70%, allowing them to retire in as few as 8.5 years.

The ultimate goal may be to save 100% of the second salary, but do what you can and work toward that goal. Remember, spend money on what brings happiness to your family and life.

6 Essential Steps to Incorporating the 60/40 Bucket System

Incorporating the 60/40 budget, or a variant of it, takes time and discipline. It will not happen overnight and should not be expected. However, if you choose to adopt this method of budgeting, here are six quick steps to follow to make it easier.

1.   Monitor your spending (for at least three months)

I recommend services such as Mint.com, Personal Capital, or You Need a Budget. Each service has a website interface along with apps for Android and iOS so that you can access your account from nearly every device you own. They also offer the option of connecting to your bank accounts to allow transactions to be automatically imported and categorized.

2. Confront your spending

At the end of the month, review the service you chose and see how much you are spending. I usually do this on a weekend, and it takes me less than 20 minutes. The results may surprise you.

I often ask people to estimate what they think they spend their money on and how much and then ask them to track their expenses to see how close they were compared to their actual spending. Usually, the estimates are way off. It is always a good thing to confront spending sooner rather than later.

The first month provides a sense of your fixed expenses, such as rent, car payments, and child care, and of your variable costs, such as entertainment. However, one month is not enough to create an accurate picture. You may have a dentist appointment one month, an oil change another, and tuition due in yet another. To obtain a more accurate average, monitor your expenses for at least three months.

3. Create financial goals

You now know your monthly fixed and discretionary expenses and how much saving on the little things adds up over time. So, put together a financial plan with goals that you can realistically achieve over the course of a year. Setting specific financial goals and working consistently to meet them can fill you with a deep sense of accomplishment in your life.

Financial goals can be categorized as short-term, medium-term, and long-term. Make a goal for each.

- **Short-term goal:** What will you do today, tomorrow, next week, and this month to start making an impact on your situation? It could be to pay down your credit card debt or cut down expenses by a certain amount.

- **Medium-term goal**: Set a goal that is at least a year away. Do you want to have an emergency fund and have a portion of your debt paid off?

- **Long-term goal:** Decide what Big Hairy Audacious Goal (BHAG) you want to accomplish with your finances over the next few years. Perhaps it is being debt-free, having a down payment on a house, or paying for your children's college tuition.

4. <u>Reduce your spending over time</u>

Now that you have your financial goals and are more mindful of your purchases, try to make small changes to reduce your expenses over time. Ask yourself if a purchase is taking away a negative. For example, if you feel tired in the morning and need a coffee, get a coffee. But instead of getting a latte at Starbucks every day, settle for a drip coffee either from home or, better still, get the free coffee at the office. These small cutbacks add up over time and give you confidence in your ability to budget.

Another method is adopting the cash diet. Essentially, you give yourself a daily budget and pay only cash for most of your expenses. One simple way to adopt this is to use envelopes. On payday, set aside a certain amount of cash in a labeled envelope for each category. When you pay cash for things, keep the receipt and put it in the envelope so that you know how much you spent on what. The underlying principle is to never borrow money from one envelope to beef up another. Leftover money can either be kept in the envelope to allow for more spending the next month or can be moved to a savings goal or for repaying debt. If you use this method, include a buffer envelope because it is likely that your expenses will vary month to month.

5. Leave buffer room

You do not want to adopt the 60/40 budget right away. Take small steps and enjoy life. Have some fun, treat your friends, but remember your goal. If you go out one weekend, be disciplined during the week.

6. Reward yourself

This might seem counterintuitive to reward yourself in reaching your financial goals, but I believe this is key when developing the habit of paying back debt. Of course, going too far with the reward can be counterproductive. If you hit a financial milestone, such as saving up 5% for a down payment for a house and your goal is a 20% payment, celebrate by going out that night.

SAVINGS TIPS

In general, do not spend more than 25% of your gross income per month on housing if you want to hit the 60/40 budgeting target. Many people are shocked that they spend close to 40% when they include costs like utilities. If you spend more than 25% of your income, find a cheaper place to live if you can. To hit the 40/60 goal, aim for housing to be 10% to 15% of your monthly income. If you rent, save the difference between your rent and what a mortgage would cost. I rented my friend's basement suite for $500 a month for over two years in the suburbs. Before that, I lived with my family for a few years in the suburbs for about the same amount. At the time, the amount was about 6% of my gross income or 11% of my after-tax income. My living expenses are now $900 a month with utilities, cable, and internet included. That might sound extreme. Only you know what you are comfortable with. You can always find a roommate to split the cost of housing or, if you have a spare bedroom, Airbnb it out for extra income. The goal is to reduce the cost of housing to as low as possible since it is the largest expense each month. But remember, live comfortably. I know many do not want to live in a sketchy part of town, and families have different space requirements. Every dollar you save adds up over time and allows you to retire earlier. One hundred dollars a month savings on rent is $1,200 a year and can grow to over $537,000[12] over 40 years in a stock index if you keep saving and investing it.

Savings Tips for Food

We all have the same number of hours in the day, but most of us are so busy at work that to come home and cook dinner, especially with a family, is a lot. Most of the time, it is easier just to order in and call it a day. With Uber Eats and SkipTheDishes, eating out has never been easier.

Step 1: Add Up Your Daily Spending on Food

Think about what it costs when using those services. The average delivery fee for Uber Eats is $4—not to mention the meal, which may cost $15, give or take a few dollars. That is nearly $20 a meal just for *dinner*. If we eat out for dinner, we likely eat out for lunch as well. So, add another $15 a day for lunch. Now, we are at $35 a day. Add a couple of coffees, and we are quickly at $40 a day. That is $200 a work week or $800 a month for food, and that is just for *one person*, not even including the weekends. Multiply that by 12 months in a year, and that is $9,600 a year on lunches and dinners during the work week. If your take-home pay is $45,000 after tax, you are spending 21% on eating out. Food costs are a significant reason why it is hard to save.

Step 2: Batch Cook to Save Time and Money

What I described above was me right after undergrad. Sure, I was saving money on my commute by taking public transportation, but I was more than making up for that by eating out. After doing that for my first year out of school, I knew there had to be a better way. Then, I read *The 4-Hour Workweek* and came across the concept of batching to be more productive. I am lazy by nature, so anything that saves me time and money is worth a try.

You can do batch cooking any day of the week, but for me, I find batch cooking on Sunday results in me doing it more often. Search for online recipes that are easy to create in batches that you can use for lunch and dinner. Favorites of mine can be made in a slow cooker, like chili, stew, and soup. I also like recipes that involve a maximum of 10 ingredients and are baked in the oven. I usually have a carb (rice or noodles), a green (broccoli or spinach), and a protein (chicken or beef) and then multiply that by 10 for the week. Cost per meal is less than $5, the bulk of that cost is from the protein. Another tip is to batch cook at a larger scale and make twenty, thirty, or forty meals and freeze them. This way you can cycle meals to avoid repetition, and you have a buffer in case you do not have time on the weekend to batch cook for the week. This is a lifesaver if you have a family.

Step 3: Shop at Costco or Sam's Club to Save Money

If you have a family, buy your groceries at Costco or Sam's Club. Even with the fees, you can save over $1,000 a year by shopping there. Otherwise, keep an eye out for sales and swap ingredients for the cheaper version if you can. I do not let sales dictate what I buy, however. If I need milk and it is not on sale, I still buy the milk. Time is money, and I do not have time to drive to multiple stores searching for the best deals.

Step 4: Research Affordable Recipes

Another good resource you can use is budgetbytes.com for delicious recipes designed for small budgets. They break down the cost per meal and serving so that you can easily budget your meals. The best part is you also know the prep and cook times so that you can plan your cooking time.

Other Ways to Save Money

I summed up a few quick ways you can save money now to achieve the 60/40 budget:

1. **There is no need to try to impress people.** The only validation you need is from your family and yourself. Remember internal versus external motivations.

2. **Try not to go shopping for shopping's sake.** If you need something, buy it. But do not wander aimlessly in a shopping mall looking to buy something.

3. **Wait until you need something before buying it.** Do not buy things "just in case."

4. **Cancel any clubs or memberships that do not directly contribute to your happiness and welfare.**

5. **Search online promo codes** for things you need or in-store coupons.

6. **Sell any possessions that you have not used in the past year.** You want to be frugal, which is having a high value to stuff ratio. If you are not using something, it is not providing value. I recommend using eBay for selling to a global audience for more niche items or Craigslist and Kijiji for local classifieds for more popular items.

7. **Buy used.** Use eBay or classified like Kijiji to find like new things for a fraction of the price.

8. **Avoid designer clothes, if you can.** You can usually find stylish clothing for less. If you must, only buy them if you are going to keep them for at least five years.

9. **Take care of your possessions.** Use them until they stop working or until the inconvenience to you is greater than the cost of replacing it. Then, toss them. Do not spend the money to move items that you are not going to use.

10. **Find a roommate, if you can.** This technique is one of the easiest and best ways to save money.

11. **Do your research on value, quality, and durability.** The cheapest item is not necessarily the best value if it is low-quality.

12. **Avoid playing the lottery.** It is a tax on the poor. Studies show that the neighborhoods that spend a lot on the lottery are the lowest income areas of town. Of course, buying the occasional ticket, if it is within your budget, does not hurt.

13. **Avoid gambling if you can.** The reason casinos exist is because the odds are in their favor. If you do gamble, give yourself a limited budget and stick to it.

14. **Do it yourself.** You can save money by doing your own taxes and changing a tire, for example. Use online tutorials to make things like this easy and cost-effective.

15. **Monitor your bank account and see if you are using the correct account.** Try to find a bank account with the lowest fees for your needs. The average American pays $329 a year in bank fees, so find a lower-fee account or an account with no fees.

16. **Take care of your body.** Medical costs in the U.S. are high, so staying healthy is good for your wallet. Exercise and eat right.

17. **Be smart with your wedding.** The average wedding cost is $28,000.

18. **Live at home for as long as you can.** Oh, and your parents can tolerate it! Offer to pay an amount to offset some expenses. You save a lot of money this way instead of rushing to move out the first chance you get. I lived at home until I was 27.

19. **Use Gasbuddy.com to save on gas.**

20. **Monitor your bills.** If something seems off, call the company to confirm the charge. For example, with my cell phone bill recently, I noticed I was paying a $15 a month fee even though I was below my data limit. By catching the mistake early, I saved $180 a year.

21. **For dental work, if you do not have the cash to pay for your copay upfront, ask to space out the treatments or negotiate payment plans with the dentist for extensive work.** It is better to make payments than to put it on your credit card where you will be charged interest unless you can pay it back within the month. Consider going to a dental school clinic where you may pay as little as a third of what a traditional dentist would cost and still receive excellent care.[13]

22. **If you own multiple vehicles, calculate if you really need the second vehicle.** If it is not being used regularly, sell it to save on costs.

23. **Take advantage of happy hour** if you are going out with friends. The cost savings will add up.

24. **Unsubscribe from email newsletters of your favorite stores.** Unfollow any brands or stores that trigger you to spend more money. Delete your credit card information from all apps and online stores to make it harder to spend.

25. **Unfollow people on social media who make you feel like you need to spend to keep up.**

26. **Negotiate your cell phone plans, insurance, and bank fees.** Shop around and compare prices. If you find a lower price, call up your provider and ask if they can match it. If they say no, say you want to be a customer but are willing to switch. For bank fees, ask if they will waive the fee. This tactic works wonders. Between getting lower rates on my cell phone plan, insurance, and bank fees, I save over $1,540 a year, which can grow to $262,581 over 30 years in the stock market, or $689,260 in 40 years.

27. **Avoid decision fatigue.** Research shows that making a lot of decisions can lead to detrimental effects on your finances. Simplify your life and automate a lot of small decisions, e.g., what to eat for breakfast or wear the next day, to be able to have the mental energy to make larger decisions. Alternatively, make your big financial decisions in the morning to avoid fatigue and making the wrong decision.

28. **Practice meditating.** Science[14] proves that meditation will increase your willpower.

29. **Develop a routine.** Routines can prevent you from becoming tempted to spending money. As Jocko Willink, ex-commander of Task Unit Bruiser, the most decorated Special Operations Unit of the Iraq War, once said, "discipline equals freedom." In this case, a routine gives you the freedom to hit your financial goals.

30. **Sign up for free customer rewards programs,** but be careful about store credit cards.

31. **Invite friends over instead of going out.**

32. **Create a visual reminder of your debt.** Put it on your fridge or somewhere you will see often. It will provide motivation.

33. **Take public transportation** if it is not too far of a commute.

34. **Cut your own hair.** This will be easier if you have a simple haircut.

35. **Use your public library to read books.** Some offer their services online, which makes it easy and convenient.

36. **Switch to term life insurance.** See Chapter 7: Have Insurance Just in Case.

37. **Bundle your insurance policies.** If you are buying auto, home/renter's, and life separately, bundle them with one company to save 10% to 20% or more for each policy bundled.

38. **Install CFL or LED lightbulbs where it makes sense.** Energy-efficient bulbs may cost more upfront but save you money over time.

39. **Take advantage of price matching.** Amazon does not always have the lowest prices, so shop around.

40. **Do your Christmas shopping on Black Friday.** I do each year and save a lot of money.

41. **Wait a day before you make a large purchase.** Impulse buying is a major reason why our savings are not where they should be.

42. **Consolidate your banking to take advantage of bundle discounts.** For example, you may get credit card fees waived if you have a mortgage with the same bank.

43. **Make your own coffee or take advantage of the office coffee maker.** You can save up to $15 a week or more.

44. **Ditch cable.** I have a Netflix subscription instead, saving over $500 a year.

45. **Cut the land line.** Having a cell phone subscription these days is more cost-effective and convenient.

46. **Avoid shopping hungry.** You are more likely to buy more junk food at the grocery store if you are hungry.

47. **Buy generic.** The product is likely the same except in price.

48. **Join the Dollar Shave Club or a similar service.** Razors are a fraction of the typical cost.

49. **Vacation off season.** I often like to travel during shoulder seasons. That way I can still take advantage of decent weather at a fraction of the price of peak season.

50. **Sign up for flight alerts to find the best deals.** The best one I saw was going from Calgary to Tokyo to Sydney round trip, business class for $1,000. Regular price would have been over $5,000.

BE FRUGAL BUT NOT CHEAP

Being frugal is different than being cheap. Being frugal means being smart with your money—doing the appropriate research, shopping around, buying used if you can, and asking yourself if you truly need that purchase. It is about having a high joy to stuff ratio. If you have 10 pairs of shoes and wear them all on a regular basis for years, you are frugal. At the same time, being frugal means being able to spend money on others when you are on a date or out with your friends. It means not being afraid of taking your buddy out for coffee or going for drinks after work. It is simply choosing the things you care about to spend money on and saving money on the rest.

The key is what you do between these experiences and ensuring they are not an everyday occurrence. Choose to selectively spend to capture those good times but live according to your financial goals when nobody is around.

Being cheap means trying to save every penny like Ebenezer Scrooge. Do not be like Scrooge. No one likes someone who is too cheap.

Cheap	Frugal
Cheap people only care about the cost of something they buy.	Frugal people care about the *value* of what they buy.
Cheap people buy the cheapest thing on the menu.	Frugal people are smart with their money, trying to get the lowest cost on things, but spend money on what they really care about.
Cheap people affect other people around them in a negative way and rarely spend money on others.	Frugal people are not afraid of spending money on people they care for.
Cheap people keep a tally of everything people owe them.	Frugal people do not keep track of what people owe them.

SUMMARY

To look toward the future, you need to make peace with your financial past. This chapter showed you how to calculate your net worth so that you know where you are starting from. It also talked about how using the bucket system for budgeting is far easier and more successful than monitoring every dollar, and how you can set financial goals and achieve them. A quick recap:

- Calculate your net worth so that you know where you are starting from.

- Keep track of your spending for three months using a budgeting app.

- Confront your spending by analyzing your expense categories.

- Create financial goals:

    - Short-term: What will you do today, tomorrow, next week, this month to start making an impact on your situation?

    - Medium-term: Set a goal that is at least a year away to aim for. Do you want to have an emergency fund and have a portion of your debt paid off?

    - Long-term: Decide what Big Hairy Audacious Goal (BHAG) you want to accomplish with your finances over the next few years. Perhaps it is being debt-free, having a down payment on a house, or paying for your children's college tuition

- Reduce your spending over time by tweaking your spending habits to achieve your goals.

- Reward yourself once you hit your financial goals.

- Adopt the 60/40 budget (or 40/60) and create the four-bucket system creating separate bank accounts for each:

- Spending Account: For daily expenses.
- Emergency Fund Account: To provide safety money. Save at least $1,000 at first, and then once you are debt-free, build it up to two months of your salary as an emergency fund.
- Savings:
  - Short-term: For the occasional splurge, vacation, and down payments.
  - Long-term: For your long-term wealth and security.
- Focus on building a $1,000 emergency fund first, and then focus on debt repayment. After that, concentrate on saving.
- Reduce your housing costs to below 25% of your income if you can for the 60/40 budget. Aim for 10% to 15% of your income for the 40/60 budget.
- Save money and time by batch cooking and looking online for recipes.
- Be frugal but not cheap.
- Negotiate to save money and increase your income.

CHAPTER THREE

SAVE 25X YOUR ANNUAL SPENDING RATE

HOW MUCH DO I NEED TO RETIRE?

The most precious resource available is not money but time. Time to do what you really want to do. And, the best way to gain time is to retire earlier. As a result, the first question people usually ask me about personal finance is, "How much money do I need to retire?"

Most financial beginners throw out numbers like $5 million to $100 million. However, the range should be more like $2 million to $10 million. In short: You need 25 times your annual *spending rate* to comfortably retire. How did I come up with that number? It is all about the 4% rule, or the 4% safe withdrawal rate.

The 4% Rule

Where did this number come from? It assumes that your return on investment for your retirement portfolio rises 7% per year minus a 3% inflation rate per year, giving you a 4% return per year in retirement. As a point of reference, the stock market has risen close to 10% a year historically.

Theoretically, if you then withdraw 4% per year for your retirement expenses, you can withdraw that amount indefinitely. In reality, however, the market moves up and down daily. Over 25 years or more during your retirement, wars, another depression, or a financial crisis could happen. You cannot predict these things in advance. So, what do you do? Some people say that you should only withdraw 2% of your retirement savings and save more than 25 times your income.

Three finance professors at Trinity University conducted the Trinity study in 1998 that showed what the maximum safe withdrawal rate would be for various retirement years between 1925-1955, 1926-1956, 1927-1957, and so on for 44 rolling periods between January 1925 and December 2009. They assumed hypothetical retirees held 50% of their assets in five-year U.S. government bonds and 50% in stocks, which is considered a conservative approach to asset allocation.

What they found is the 4% withdrawal rate is the worst-case scenario.[*15] People could have withdrawn 5% quite safely without a decrease in their asset value 20 times out of the 30-year period, meaning a 67% success rate. Withdrawing 4% a year would have yielded a 96% success rate. That being said, criticism around the 4% rule exists, namely:

- The Trinity study does not include mutual fund fees. Depending on the mutual fund, you can pay up to 1% to 2% in fees per year. This adds up to a lot of fees over time.

- The Trinity study considers retirement lengths of up to 30 years. If you retire early, you will likely be retired longer than 30 years.

- The 4% rule has not held up as well in other developed countries as it has in the U.S.

- The Trinity study does not assume that retirees plan to bequeath an estate.
- The Trinity study does not consider taxes to be paid on the withdrawn money.

Mr. Money Mustache's response to those criticisms is that the Trinity study was ultraconservative in their assumptions, assuming retirees **never**:

- Work another day in their life, either through part-time employment or a side business.
- Collect from a pension plan.
- Adjust their spending to account for changes in the economy.
- Change their spending habits to compensate for price increases.
- Collect inheritance.
- Deviate from their portfolio allocation of 50% stocks and 50% bonds.
- And never do what studies have shown most old people do—spend less as they age.

I will add that the Trinity study:
- Does not consider the ability to move to a less expensive location.
- Does not consider Medicare health insurance coverage in the U.S.

Both our points are that the Trinity study assumes that the income you make stops the second you retire and that expenses and your financial situation stay constant throughout your retirement. Many retirees continue to pursue passions and often have side gigs. A million ways exist to make money in retirement, and chances are that you will adjust your spending as you get older as well. The Trinity study should, therefore, be considered conservative in its assumptions.

WHEN CAN I RETIRE?

The simple answer is: When you have saved 25 times your annual spending rate. What is your **spending rate**? It is everything that comes out of your paycheck, bank account, credit cards, and automatic payments. I suggest including property taxes and sales taxes but do not count income taxes or other payroll taxes. I also recommend excluding all loan interest, principal payments, and retirement contributions when calculating your spending rate. Why? Because once you become financially independent you will not have loans to pay off, and once retired, you will probably be in a lower income tax bracket and no longer contribute to your retirement account.

Let's break down the spending rate with an example:

Gross Income: $5,000 a month or $60,000 a year
Monthly Expenses:

- Food: $618

- Entertainment: $500

- Utilities: $80

- Car Insurance: $93

- Gas: $127

- Cable: $99

- Cellphone: $50

- Miscellaneous: $200

Monthly expenses=

$618 + $500 + $80 + $93 + $127 + $99 + 50 + $200= $1,767

Yearly expenses=

$1,767 x 12 months= $21,204

Money needed to retire=

$$\$21,204 \textbf{ x } 25 \text{ years} = \$530,100$$

It seems we would need to save $530,100 to be able to retire, but that is not entirely correct. Our kids will hopefully have moved out, and our everyday expenses will likely decrease. However, we will probably be traveling and spending money on other pursuits, offsetting our reduced spending. So, let's use the numbers above and calculate the savings rate to determine how long it will take to save that amount.

The **savings rate** is the percentage of your take-home pay that you set aside as a nest egg for retirement. The savings rate is primarily focused on any long-term savings you may be making.

To calculate your savings rate is easy. Take your gross paycheck and subtract all taxes. This number is your **take-home pay**. Subtract your spending, and you now have your savings. Note, contributions to a 401(k) or other savings plan should not be counted as an expense. Add back any employer matching 401(k) contributions and divide this by your take-home pay to determine your savings rate.

Savings rate=

((take-home pay - spending)/take-home pay) x 100

Take-home pay=

gross paycheck - taxes + 401(k) employer contributions

Take home pay in the above example:

Gross Pay: $5,000 a month

- 401(k): $400
- Employer 401(k) Match: $175
- Automatic deduction for student loans: $300
- Automatic deduction for car loans: $300

- Federal tax (at 25%): $1,250
- State tax (at 8%): $400

Take-home pay=

$5,000 + $175 - $300 - $300 - $1,250 - $400= $2,925

Savings rate=

(($2,925 - $1,767)/$2,925) x 100= 40%

It would take 22 years to save[16] the money needed to retire, assuming we invest our current savings at a 5% annual return rate.

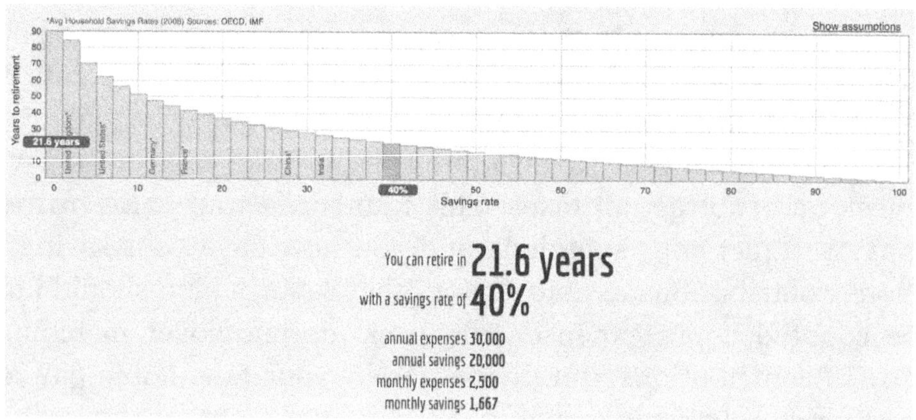

You might be thinking: Well, that is assuming we make the same amount every year without a promotion or raise. Correct. But you would be surprised by how quickly our lifestyle adapts to increased earnings—new car, house, clothes, iPhone, watch. This is called lifestyle inflation. The more important factor here is not how much we spend but how much we SAVE. Think about it: If you cut out an expense, you are not only saving money this year, you are saving money indefinitely. Suddenly, spending $99 a month on cable does not seem like a good idea, when over 20 years that is equal to $23,760.

Savings over 1 year=

$99 x 12 months= $1,188

Savings over 20 years=

$1,188 x 20 years= $23,760

Using the above example, eliminating that one expense increases our savings rate by $1,188 a year or 3.4%, meaning we can retire **1.8 YEARS FASTER!**

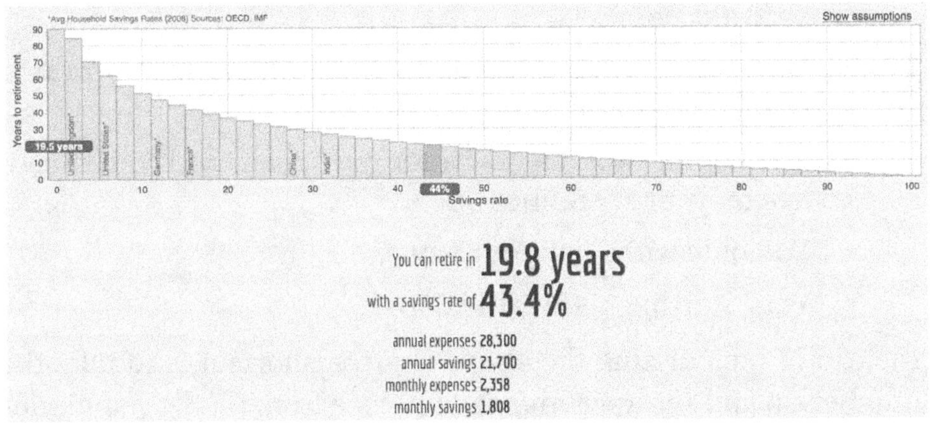

If you want a rough guideline as to what savings rate is needed to retire, this chart puts things into perspective:

Savings Rate vs. Working Years Until Retirement[17]

Savings Rate (Percent)	Working Years Until Retirement
5	66
10	51
15	43
20	37
25	32
30	28
35	25
40	22
45	19
50	17
55	14.5
60	12.5
65	10.5

70	8.5
75	7
80	5.5
85	4
90	3
95	2
100	1

Assumptions:

- You earn 5% investment returns during your working years, inflation-adjusted.

- You withdraw 4% a year after retirement and continue to live on your spending rate.

- You only withdraw your gains.

- Your starting net worth is $0.

Instead of memorizing the above chart, a shortcut is to take the number 60 and subtract your savings rate from it. The remainder is roughly how long you need to work before you have enough savings to support yourself in retirement, assuming you start with zero net worth. This calculation breaks down with savings rates over 40%. So, if you save more than that, subtract from 70.

Years needed to retire with a savings rate of 40% or less=
60 - 30% savings rate= ~30 years

Years needed to retire with a savings rate of greater than 40%=
70 - 50% savings rate= ~20 years

Note: Historically U.S. stocks have increased 9.7% per year or 7% after adjusting for inflation. The 5% returns in the examples above are conservative estimates and assume a mixed stock/bond portfolio.

THE POWER OF SAVING VS. SPENDING

Contrary to what people think, income is not equal to financial stability. In other words, how much money a person makes does not determine if they will be financially stable or not. Let's use the following comparison between a dentist[18] and a receptionist[19] living in San Francisco using average salary levels as of March 2018.

Carl, the Dentist

- Carl, 38 years old, is doing quite well for himself, pulling in $184,000 last year. Originally from Seattle, he recently moved to San Francisco to set up a new practice. Even though real estate is expensive, he wanted to be close to work, so he rented a 2-bedroom apartment in the prestigious Marina district. The view from his place is unreal. He can see the Bay and the Golden Gate bridge and walk to Fisherman's Wharf. Carl is living the dream. His rent payment is $5,000 a month.

- He drives to work in his 2017 Cadillac Escalade, which he leases for $1,170 per month. He pays an additional $300 in car insurance.

- He loves to eat out at the nicest restaurants with his wife, paying $1,000 a month for food.

- He frequently entertains at his place and has a healthy red wine habit. Entertainment expenses are $1,000 a month.

- Carl and his wife share the same credit card, often spending more when traveling than they can afford. On average, they pay $300 a month toward credit card debt.

- Dental school was not cheap, so Carl continues to make student loan payments of $300 a month.

- Utilities are normally $350 a month, which consists of power, gas, water, broadband, and two cell phone connections.

- Fortunately, his wife stays at home with the kids, so he does not have to pay for childcare.

Joe, the Receptionist

- Joe, 22 years old, recently graduated and landed a job at the new dental clinic near the Golden Gate Bridge in San Francisco.

- He moved in with a friend in the Panhandle neighborhood, near the University of San Francisco. His portion of the rent is $750 a month.

- He drives around in his 2007 Honda Civic, which he has been driving since high school. Other than maintenance and oil changes, it has not caused him any issues. He pays $100 a month for car insurance.

- He likes eating out but mostly for special occasions. Joe spends his Sunday afternoons meal prepping so that he has easy-to-eat lunches and dinners during the week. He keeps his food costs low, at $200 a month.

- Joe bikes a lot using the city bike lanes but likes to take road trips down to Mountain View and San Jose to visit friends. He spends about $120 a month on gas.

- Joe likes going out with his friends as his primary source of entertainment. He spends $300 a month on this.

- Joe also likes to travel but looks for good flight deals and stays in hostels to keep costs down. Usually, he can pay off his travel expenses using his savings, so he does not have any credit card debt.

- Joe is also paying off his student loans, making $150 payments per month. He has no other debt.

- Utilities are about $150 a month, which consists of power, broadband, and one cell phone connection.

Income	Carl, the Dentist	Joe, the Receptionist
Annual Income	$184,000	$42,577
Standard Deduction	$12,000	$12,000
Taxable Income	**$172,000**	**$30,577**
Federal Income Tax	$36,730	$3,479
California State Income Tax	$15,368	$1,220
Social Security	$7,886	$2,640
Medicare Tax	$2,668	$617
Total Tax	**$62,652**	**$7,956**
Annual Take-Home Pay	$121,348	$34,621
Monthly Take-Home Pay	**$10,112**	**$2,885**

Expenses	Carl	Joe
Mortgage or Rent	$5,000	$750
Food	$1,000	$200
Car Insurance	$300	$100
Gas	$200	$120
Credit Card Payments	$300	$0
Car/Lease Payment	$1,170	$0
Student Loan Payment	$300	$150
Entertainment	$1,000	$300
Utilities	$350	$150
Total Expenses	**$9,620**	**$1,770**
Savings per month	**$492 or 4.9%**	**$1,115 or 38.6%**

*Based on 2018 U.S. single filing status rates using taxformcalculator.com

Carl has it all—a new house in a prestigious area, the latest luxury SUV, traveling in style, enjoying the pleasures of the upper-middle-class life. He is not too worried about saving since he has a stable job and figures he can always save later when his kids are grown. He does not have an emergency fund because he knows he can just throw the expense on his credit card.

Joe, on the other hand, makes below the median[20] household income in the U.S. He might even be considered poor by Carl's standards. And, Joe certainly would not be able to afford to buy a home in San Francisco with his current salary. Most months, he saves close to 40%, but unexpected costs pop up, which is why he has a $1,000 emergency fund in a separate bank account. Fortunately, he read this book and modeled his expenses after the spending bucket concept in Chapter 2: Know Where Your Money Is Going. He puts everything else into his investment account and invests in a stock/ bond split, like the allocation in the Trinity study.

Who is more financially stable? Carl saves only 4.9% of his monthly take home, while Joe saves 38.6%. The $623 a month savings difference is staggering. If Carl and Joe continue to save money at their respective saving rates, Joe can comfortably retire in 23 years, by age 45. His investment portfolio will be worth $582,057 by then, assuming a 5% annual return using the Trinity study assumption. Using the 4% withdrawal rule, he would be able to live on $23,282 or $1,940 a month, slightly more than what he spends today.

Savings over 23 years=
$1,115 x 12 months x 23 years x (1 + 89.139% compound interest)= $582,057

Money needed for Joe's retirement (25x yearly spending rate)=
$1,115 x 12 months x 23 years= $307,740 in savings
+
$274,317 in interest= $582,057

4% yearly withdrawal=
$582,057 x 4%= $23,282.28

4% monthly withdrawal=
$23,282.28 / 12 months= $1,940.19

Carl, on the other hand, would be able to retire in 66 years. Let's assume, however, that he cuts back his spending in retirement and is debt-free by age 65. His portfolio would be worth $338,905. Using the 4% withdrawal rule, he would have to live on $13,556 a year or $1,030 a month, 10.2% of his take-home pay during his working years. Something tells me he will not be able to retire fully at age 65 and will continue to work to support himself well past then.

Savings over 27 years=
$$\$492 \text{ x } 12 \text{ months x } 27 \text{ years x}$$
$$(1+ 112.602\% \text{ compound interest})= \$338,905$$

4% yearly withdrawal=
$$\$338,905 \text{ x } 4\%= \$13,556.20$$

4% monthly withdrawal=
$$\$13,556.20 \text{ / } 12 \text{ months}= \$1,129.68$$

Joe can retire at age 45, while Carl must wait until age 65 and still will have a fraction of a nest egg. Even with Joe making $140,000+ less per year than Carl, who would you rather be?

The above example is used for simplicity. It is likely that Joe and Carl will make more money over time, but hopefully, they put that earning potential into savings rather than increase expenses. It also assumes that neither has an unexpected major emergency and each withdraws 4% of their income in retirement. If they invested in an S&P 500 index fund, their returns would have averaged 9.7% per year, not 5% per year.

SUMMARY

Remember the 4% rule and save 25 times your annual spending. It is a very conservative metric and meant as a guiding post to help you save. The beauty of this rule is that it is flexible, and there is little difference between a 30-year period and infinity. If you spend less money, you can retire on less. It is one of the most important concepts in this book.

Another important concept to remember is that it is not how much you earn but how much you save. It is possible to be able to retire faster making $40,000 a year than someone making $100,000 a year. The key is that the more you cut back on non-essential expenses, the more you can save, and the faster you can retire. Who would you rather be, Carl, the Dentist, or Joe, the Receptionist? Do not cut back so much that you do not enjoy life. The point is to spend on things that maximize your happiness while cutting back on things that do not add to it.

- Calculate your monthly expenses, take-home pay, and savings rate.

- Once you know the years until retirement, decide if that is soon enough. If not, reduce your expenses or increase your income using a side hustle to save more.

CHAPTER FOUR

BUILD A SMALL EMERGENCY FUND

WHY YOU NEED AN EMERGENCY FUND

Bankrate's January 2018 Financial Security Index survey stated that 34% of American households experienced a major unexpected expense over the past year. However, only 39% of survey respondents said they would be able to cover a $1,000 setback using their savings. How can anyone afford to save if they cannot afford a $1,000 setback? People need emergency funds. Personal finance expert Dave Ramsey says, "It's crucial to have an emergency fund because it prevents a twist in the track from completely derailing the journey."

Many reasons exist to avoid emergency savings, such as purchasing something we want, paying down our debt, or investing it in the stock market. But it is one of the most crucial things you need to do to get your finances in order. If you prefer to invest that money consider this: What if you invest $1,000 and your investments are at a low when an emergency happens? You are going to lose money.

An emergency fund is not a waste of resources. Having an emergency fund is vitally important, so I strongly recommend creating an emergency fund over paying down debt, and I explain that reasoning later in this chapter. It is better to keep some money **liquid** for a rainy day. Liquid means easy access to your money without incurring penalties.

The most liquid asset is cash, so I suggest opening a separate bank account and storing it there. Because having cash on hand is so accessible, you might be tempted to spend this money. To mitigate this temptation, open an account at another bank so that the funds are out of sight and out of mind.

You might be wondering, "Are credit cards a form of emergency fund?" Yes, and no. Depending on the emergency, you might not be able to pay off the balance of your credit card. I strongly urge you to avoid payday loans at all costs, however.

Some of the most common financial emergencies people face and why an emergency fund is recommended:[21]

1. Job Loss

This is the primary reason for an emergency fund. If you lose your job and do not have a cash cushion, your credit card debt could spiral out of control in no time.

2. Major Health Expenses

Unexpected health expenses still require you to pay the deductible, even if you have health insurance.

3. Major Dental Expenses

A lot of dental plans have limitations on the amount they cover. People with dental insurance commonly have what is described as "100-80-50" coverage, meaning the insurance company pays 100% of the cost of routine preventive and diagnostic care, like cleanings and checkups; 80% for fillings, root canals, and other basic procedures; and 50% for crowns, bridges, and major procedures.[22]

Most dental plans also max out at $1,500 a year, which is only a fraction of the cost of your kid's $6,000 braces. Even fillings and root canals can cost you hundreds of dollars. Having an emergency fund will help cover any dental costs.

4. Emergency Pet Care

You might be able to afford the everyday expenses of owning a pet, but are you prepared for thousands of dollars in vet bills? If you own a breed of dog that is susceptible to health issues, I recommend pet insurance, but you will still be on the hook for deductibles.

5. Car Repairs

Whether replacing your tires, brakes, cracked windshield, battery, or damage from an accident, you want spare cash to cover car repairs.

6. Home Repairs

Have homeowner's insurance for major expenses, but you must first pay the deductible. And insurance does not cover everything that can go wrong. For example, your balcony might need replacing but may not be covered by insurance.

7. Larger Than Expected Tax Bill

Unexpected taxes can come due during tax time. Be prepared with an emergency fund so that you avoid paying any late penalties. In the U.S., that means 5% of the taxes owed for every month, up to a maximum of 25%. If you file more than 60 days after the due date, the minimum penalty is $205 or 100% of your unpaid tax, whichever is less.

In Canada, late penalties are 5% of your balance owing plus 1% of your balance owing for each full month your return is late to a maximum of 12 months, or 17% a year.[23] The real kicker is if you have been charged a late filing penalty in any of the three previous tax years, then your penalty for the current year is double. This means paying 10% of your balance owing, plus 2% per month to a max of 20 months or *50%*. Ouch! That hurts the wallet. Having an emergency fund prevents you from having to deal with potential late penalties.

8. Unanticipated Travel

A death in the family can force you to purchase a last-minute plane ticket to go to the funeral. You do not want this expense lingering on your credit card, racking up interest.

9. Funerals

Funerals can cost over $10,000. If your loved one had life insurance, this might cover the cost of the funeral. Often, it takes months to receive reimbursement, so you will need a source of cash to make the payment.

Beyond financial stability, other advantages to having an emergency reserve of cash are that:

- It helps lower your stress level.

- It keeps you from spending frivolously.

- It prevents you from making bad financial decisions.

Why Build an Emergency Fund Over Paying Debt?

This may seem counterintuitive at first. You are putting money into an emergency fund, but you still have debt to pay. Shouldn't you pay your debt first and then build an emergency fund? Think of it this way: Say you throw 100% of every dollar toward debt repayment and do not have a spare dollar left at the end of the month. Things are going smoothly, but then BAM, you need a new transmission. Where are you going to get the money to pay for that? It is going right back on your credit card, and you have not gotten ahead. Psychologically this feels like defeat.

If you build a small emergency fund first, like $1,000, which you can build up faster than a larger fund of say six months, then it can help keep you from derailing your financial goals. Once you have a $1,000 fund and have your debts paid off, increase this fund to two months' worth of salary. Any emergencies that go beyond your two-month fund can be funded using **springy debt**. Springy debt is debt you can pay off or increase at will. A credit card is one form (although not ideal), and a line of credit is another (better) option. The important thing is to keep this debt at a zero balance until you have an emergency or another circumstance that requires you to draw on it.

BUILDING AN EMERGENCY FUND

Three main strategies for building an emergency fund:

- **The prioritization method:** This strategy makes your emergency fund your #1 priority. Every spare dollar you have builds it up until it is complete.

- **The "take advantage of windfalls" method**: This approach uses things like bonuses, inheritances, and gifts to build up your emergency fund.

- **Percentage-based emergency savings method:** This process takes a percentage of your monthly income and builds up your fund over time.

I advocate the prioritization or percentage-based methods. In either case, you make creating an emergency fund a part of your budget, whereas with the "take advantage of windfalls" method, you wait for funds that you may or may not receive.

As for building an emergency fund, there are 4 steps I recommend:

Step 1: Open a High-Interest (or "High-Yield") Savings Account for Your Emergency Fund

The first step is to open a high-interest or high-yield savings account for your emergency fund. A high-interest savings account, as the name suggests, pays higher interest than standard savings accounts. Unlike checking accounts, which are meant for daily transactions, high-interest savings accounts are designed to hold money over a longer period—perfect for an emergency fund. Research the accounts offered at your current financial institution, but also look at alternative accounts. If you live in the U.S., use

Nerdwallet.com to find the highest-interest savings accounts. In Canada, look at Ratehub.ca. You can find interest rates between 1.4% and 2.3%, much better than the 0.05% interest rates on regular savings accounts.[24]

A few things to consider when opening a high-interest savings account:

- **Interest rates:** Also known as APY. The higher, the better.

- **Fees:** See what the fees are. Try to find accounts with low or no fees as the entire purpose is to save money.

- **Number of transactions permitted:** While you are unlikely to make a lot of transactions with an emergency fund, ensure that the number on the account is enough for your needs.

- **Accessing the funds:** What options are available to withdraw funds? Can you write checks? Transfer funds electronically? Use an ATM? The easier you can access the funds, the better. In an emergency, you will need the money quickly.

Step 2: Build an Emergency Fund Using an Automatic Savings Plan

Start with a $1,000 emergency fund. This initial $1,000 will build a buffer between unexpected life events that will most likely pop up. The last thing you want is something like getting a flat tire and going further into debt. Moreover, $1,000 is an achievable target and will build your confidence to save money.

The easiest way to start is to have money automatically withdrawn from each paycheck and funneled into a separate savings account. Before you know it, you will have enough money saved up for an emergency.

Step 3: Pay Off Your Debts

Once you have a $1,000 emergency fund, focus your attention on your debt, starting with the highest interest debt first, known as the "Debt Avalanche" method.

Step 4: Build Up Your Emergency Fund to Two Months and Use Springy Debt Instead of a Large Cash Cushion

Many personal finance experts suggest having three to six months of living expenses (or more) in an emergency fund. I do not necessarily agree with this strategy as long as you have a small cash cushion to keep your life running smoothly in the event of losing a job or encountering a big unexpected expense. I recommend saving a minimum of two months' worth of salary after first starting with $1,000 and then paying off your debt. I consider anything more a waste of potential earnings. I loathe keeping excess money in a savings account when it could be working for me in some investment.

The solution is to use springy debt. As previously mentioned, springy debt is debt you can easily draw on like a line of credit. The most important thing is to keep this at a zero balance and use it only in an emergency.

The critique to this view is that lines of credit and credit cards can be turned off by the bank. Critics argue that it is better to have a larger stash of cash in an emergency fund versus using springy debt. However, the way I see it is there is little chance of the bank closing your credit card and line of credit if you are making payments. The only caveat is if you lose your job, then your two months of salary savings will get you by. If you have been following my advice in this book, your spending rate should only be 60% of your monthly income, meaning your two-month salary savings will last you 2.8 months. Not to mention that you would probably cut back on non-critical expenses under these circumstances, meaning your two-month salary emergency fund could last you three to four months, around the average time it takes to find another job.[25]

SUMMARY

Prioritize having a $1,000 emergency fund over anything else, including paying down your debt. The buffer will build your confidence and allow you to handle any financial hiccup that may come, without derailing your debt repayment progress later.

- Open a high-interest savings account for your emergency fund. It is important to get as much interest as you can from your accounts, while simultaneously keeping your emergency fund liquid in case you need to use it. Do not invest this money in the stock market.

- Use an automatic savings plan to achieve your emergency fund goal effortlessly.

- Once you have $1,000 saved up, focus on debt repayment. Make this your number one priority.

- After your debt is paid off, build up your emergency fund to two months' worth of salary.

- Use springy debt instead of a large cash cushion for any unexpected expenses that go beyond what you saved in your emergency fund.

- Focus on putting the rest of your savings into index fund ETFs and watch your retirement nest egg grow.

CHAPTER FIVE

TAKE BACK CONTROL OF YOUR DEBT

FOCUS ON YOUR CREDIT CARD DEBT FIRST

During my undergrad, I was hesitant to use my credit card. Not making much money and facing a large student loan debt, I was scared to fall further into debt. I used my debit card almost exclusively, saving my credit card for the odd purchase that was above my debit card limit and immediately transferred funds to pay it off. I am not exactly sure where I developed this mentality, but I have a feeling my tough upbringing had something to do with it.

The truth is many of us spend our lives in debt. More specifically, credit card debt. Average credit card debt per household is now more than $7,000. Total debt is worse. As I mentioned in the introduction, the average American has about $12,000 in debt, not including mortgage debt. And, the average student has $20,000 of debt at graduation. It is no one's fault. Stores offer promotions to receive a discount if you apply for a card right then. Banks give away pre-qualified credit cards through the mail. It should be no surprise that the average American has four credit cards.

It is in the lender's best interest if you keep a balance on that credit card and are charged obscenely high interest rates. High-interest debt can and will grow so fast that it can overwhelm you and your other investments. This often means it makes sense to prioritize paying down your credit card debt. The average credit card has about a 15% interest rate, whereas store credit cards often charge above 20%. Paying off high-interest debt first is probably the best return you will ever see. When you start paying down your credit cards, you produce an immediate 15% to 25% return in your pocket. Remember: The stock market averages just under 10% per year.

To pay back your debt, start by paying more than the minimum payment each month. About a third of Americans pay only the minimum payment each month. Another third vacillate between paying part of the balance off one month, and then the minimum the next month. Why do so many of us only pay the minimum? For one, the credit card company says it is okay. And, we know just paying the minimum should not affect our credit score. As for what the minimum payment is, each credit card is different, but often it is $25, or 1% to 2% of the balance, plus interest and fees, whichever is greater.[26] In Canada, minimum payments are typically $10 plus the interest and fees.[27]

The reality is the minimum payment is set in such a way that if you had a $3,000 credit card balance and were making the $80 minimum payment each month (1% balance + interest), it would take you 226 months to pay off the entire debt, **which is about 19 years!**

Let's look at what paying the minimum payment and double the minimum payment saves in interest.

Credit Card Balance: $3,000	Carl	Joe
Monthly Payment	$80 (minimum)	$160 (minimum x 2)
Pay-Off Time	18 years, 10 months	1 year, 11 months
Interest Paid	$4,390.04	$627.24

*assuming 19.99% APR

You would save $3,762.80 by doubling the monthly minimum payment.

The above example also assumes that you spend no more on the card, even if your credit limit increases, which is something credit card companies often do. It is easy to become trapped in an endless debt cycle if you only make the minimum payments.

Know When Your Credit Card Payment Is Due

With credit cards, you have at least 21 days from the day the billing cycle closes to pay your bill without incurring the interest charge. If you pay your credit card entirely, it is like receiving an interest-free loan and collecting rewards, if your credit card offers those. If you miss a full payment, you are paying the interest rate on the outstanding balance. If you skip a payment, make a late payment, or pay part of the minimum payment, you incur extra charges.

<u>Credit Cards Can Be Good</u>

If you pay off your balance every month, credit cards allow you to earn rewards and save you from needing to either carry cash at all times or using your debit card, which offers no rewards and can include its own fees. Furthermore, having a credit card makes it easier to track your spending habits online and offers additional benefits, such as extended warranties and travel insurance. Two or three credit cards, say a Visa and a MasterCard, with manageable credit limits are the most you should have. Make sure no more than one has an annual fee.

Why have two or three cards? If a store does not accept Visa or MasterCard, then you will have a backup. Also, if one is stolen or compromised, you still have access to a card. Avoid those credit card offers you receive in the mail. Only apply for a credit card if you need it, however.

Be aware that 60% of people do not pay off their credit cards every month. If you have a credit card, pay off the balance *every* month. Did you know that people typically spend 47% more when using credit instead of cash? This also includes debit cards. Why? Paper is real, and we feel a tangible sense of loss using it to pay. Psychologically, when you pay with cash, you tend to spend less. If you find you spend more because you use a card instead of cash, either lower your credit limit or cancel your cards and pay with cash.

What if you do not have enough savings or emergency fund and have to carry a balance for something you absolutely need? In these circumstances, see if you can get a line of credit with a lower interest rate. Or, put it on your card and pay off your balance within three months or sooner. If you think it will take longer than three months to pay off your credit card or line of credit, then you cannot afford it.

Important: Three months of interest on a credit card is equivalent to about 7% depending on the card, almost equal to a full year of gains in the stock market. Seriously question if the purchase is worth it and if you need to carry a balance at all.

Credit Cards Can Be Bad

Stay within your credit limit. Banks often charge a hefty fee if you go over your limit, assuming your credit card transaction was not denied.

Do not use your credit card for cash advances. Most credit cards can be used to take cash out from the ATM. But when you do this, the issuers charge even higher interest rates on this amount and/or fees. Moreover, most cash advances do not have a grace period, so interest starts accruing the second you take out the cash.

Again, carrying a balance is very detrimental to your personal finances. Aim for a zero balance each month.

A basic, cash-back or travel rewards card offers 1% to 2% back. Chances are you will only spend enough during the year earning rewards to make it worth having only one card. If the rewards are less than what you are paying in annual fees, switch all your cards to no annual fee cards.

Other cards offer more on groceries, gas, travel, and dining out. Matching your spending to the highest reward category maximizes the cash back you earn on every dollar spent. Use this strategy only if you are experienced with credit cards and pay off the balance monthly. Paying interest nullifies the benefits of earning rewards.

Be Aware of the No Monthly Payments Promotions

You might be tempted by the following:

"Don't pay for 12 months. No monthly payments. 0% interest!"

"12-month financing. Pay no interest for 12 months with equal payments on all purchases."

"Employee pricing on all vehicles!"

You have probably seen ads like these. In the fine print, the interest rates are equal to or greater than most credit cards, especially if you do not pay the balance within the time frame they advertise. Be careful about store credit cards. Even with those "10% off now" promotions, they often have higher interest rates than standard credit cards. Over time, this can cost you more than the savings you receive with your purchase.

KNOW YOUR CREDIT SCORE

You may think that only credit card companies, mortgage lenders, and car dealerships care about your credit score. Unfortunately, this is not the case. Potential landlords may run a credit check to look for red flags, like a history of missed payments or a heavy debt load relative to your income. Employers may pull credit reports, which are not the same as a credit score, to see if you manage your finances well and verify your identity.

Between credit scores and credit reports, credit scores garner more attention. Your **credit score** is a number that lenders use to judge your ability to pay them back and as a crucial factor in determining interest rates on your debts. A good score allows you to receive the best deals on everything from credit cards to mortgages. A bad one can potentially cost you tens of thousands of dollars in additional interest. The difference in interest rates can be huge, especially on mortgages. Check myFico.com's loan savings calculator to determine how much a good score can save you on interest. It can be well over a 1.5% difference on a 30-year mortgage, which translates to $100,000 in interest savings with a top score versus the lowest score on a $300,000 mortgage.

To understand credit scores, you first must understand **credit reports**. These are created by credit bureaus that gather information from a range of credit card companies, lenders, and merchants with whom you have done business. Included in each report is the date you opened each account, how much you owe, your credit limits, and your payment history. Your report also indicates whether you have had major financial problems, like defaulting on a loan or declaring personal bankruptcy. It shows any requests for your credit history by third parties like landlords, employers, and lenders. All this information from your credit report is plugged into a mathematical formula to create your credit score. Every time you apply for a new loan or credit card, credit bureaus supply your credit report or credit score, sometimes both.

How Your Credit Score Is Calculated

The most common type of credit score is called the FICO score, named for the Fair Isaac Corporation, which created it. It is also referred to as a Beacon score. There are 5 important factors when determining your credit score:

1. Payment history – 35% of your score
2. How much you owe – 30%
3. Length of your credit history – 15%
4. Mix of credit – 10%
5. Number of credit applications you have – 10%

Most FICO scores range from 300 to 850. The higher the number, the better. The average score is 700, and your goal should be in the 700+ club. This is the breakdown of the scores:

- 800+: Exceptional credit
- 750 to 799: Excellent credit
- 700 to 749: Good credit
- 640 to 699: Fair credit
- 580 to 639: Poor credit
- Below 580: Bad credit

Three major credit bureaus maintain your credit reports in the U.S.: Equifax, Experian, and TransUnion. You are legally entitled to one free credit report per year from each. Everyone should know what their credit score is. To find out, go to AnnualCreditReport.com or CreditKarma.com. If you are in Canada, CreditKarma.ca is a useful resource, and some Canadian banks offer free credit score services.

Improving Your Credit Score

Surprisingly, your net worth and salary have no impact on your credit score. If you have a below-average credit score, or just want to improve it, follow these tips:

- Automate your payments. Payment history makes up the largest portion of the credit score at a 35% weighting, so making payments on time will have the biggest effect.

- Owe less than what you can potentially borrow. In other words, avoid having your credit cards and lines of credit maxed out. This is another 30% of your score, so it will have a big effect as well.

- Once you pay your debt, do not close the account. Credit history is another 15%.

- Have different kinds of debt. Having a mix of credit is another 10% of your score. For example, people with top scores have a mix of debt, like student loans, credit cards, and car loans.

- Do not apply for multiple credit applications within a short time. Every time you apply for a loan or credit card, it is noted on your credit report as an inquiry. If an employer or landlord checks your score, this is deemed a "soft" inquiry, which will not hurt your score. If a lender or credit card issuer checks your report, however, this qualifies as a "hard" inquiry. Having too many of those can negatively impact your score temporarily.

- Maintain a low **utilization ratio**, which is your actual debt versus the potential debt you could borrow. Let's say you have two credit cards, each with a $4,000 limit. You have a potential debt of $8,000. You owe $3,000 on one card and $1,000 on the other, for an actual debt of $4,000. You have a utilization ratio of 50%. If you pay off the credit card with the $1,000 balance and close it, your utilization ratio will increase to 75% since you now have a $3,000 balance with a $4,000 limit.

<u>What if I Missed a Bill and It Is in Collections?</u>

Having a bill in collections is the fastest way to destroy your credit rating. According to a 2014 Consumer Financial Protection Bureau (CFPB) report, an estimated 43 million Americans have medical debt in collections. This does not include delinquent car payments, cell phone bills, missed utility bills, or unpaid student loans.

Unfortunately, the credit bureau has a zero-tolerance policy on bills in collections, so your score will take an immediate 70 to 100-point hit. You are essentially saying, "I do not care about paying my bills on time." They do not listen to excuses. Once a bill is in collections, your first priority should be to pay it back.

Fortunately, your delinquent bill may eventually roll off your credit report, but it will take 7 or 10 years.

- **Foreclosures**: Removed from your credit report after 7 years
- **Chapter 13 bankruptcy**: Removed after 7 years
- **Chapter 7 bankruptcy**: Removed after 10 years from the filing date
- **Civil judgments**: Removed after 7 years
- **Unpaid tax liens**: May be removed after 10 years from the filing date but could stay on indefinitely
- **Paid tax liens**: Removed after 7 years from the paid date

4 STEPS TO MANAGING YOUR DEBTS

Now that you know what your credit score is and how important it is, the next thing is to devise a plan on conquering your debt. Follow these 4 steps:

Step 1: Calculate Your Debt

List all your debts except your mortgage from highest interest rate to lowest, including those with zero percent interest rates. Typically, credit cards will be at the top of the list. I recommend listing the following:

1. Amount owed to each creditor
2. Interest rate
3. Potential fees for each loan

This should all be found on either your online banking platform or through the budgeting platform you chose. A spreadsheet with the following headings can help you organize your debts:

Name of debt	Total Amount of Debt	APR	Monthly Minimum Payment

Step 2: Negotiate

Try negotiating with your credit card company to lower the rate. The worst they can say is no. However, they would prefer that you continue making some payment every month over having to collect in bankruptcy. If you pay your balance off entirely each month, then you do not have to negotiate for a lower rate since you are already paying 0%.

Step 3: Consolidate

The next thing is to find a credit card with lower interest rates on sites like CreditCards.com and CardHub.com and transfer your credit card balance to consolidate your debt. If you are Canadian, look up Greedyrates.ca and RateSuperMarket.ca.

If you have access to a line of credit or home equity line and have credit card debt, then use your lower-interest debt to pay off your higher-interest debt. Your goal is to become debt-free, but in the meantime, this is an effective way of saving money on interest payments. If you use a home equity line, be aware that if you fall behind on payments, you could put your house at risk.

Warning: If you look at a company that specializes in debt management to consolidate your debts, they could either be increasing the time to pay off your debt, to give the illusion you are paying less interest, or have a higher interest rate than your existing debt.

Do not confuse debt consolidation with debt settlements. **Debt settlements** are done by a debt counselor who negotiates on your behalf to settle your debt. They typically charge high fees and sometimes leave you worse off than when you began.

Step 4: Eliminate Your Debt

Not all debt is created equal. Lines of credit, student loans, credit cards, a home equity line on your house, or payday loans each have different terms and conditions and, most importantly, interest rates. Consider these two recommended debt elimination methods:

<u>The Debt Snowball Method</u>

Dave Ramsey, a popular American money management author, is a big proponent of the "Debt Snowball" method. This method consists of ranking the debts from smallest balance to highest and focusing on the smallest balance first. The idea is that you gain confidence over time by paying off debts in full. It also goes by the "momentum method" moniker. I do not agree with this approach. Why would you pay off a debt with zero percent interest rate before paying off your credit card with the highest interest rate? You should not gain confidence from such a mistake. Focus on your credit cards first, assuming they have the highest interest rates, then work down the list. That leads us to my preferred approach to tackling debt.

The Debt Avalanche Method

This is tackling your debt with the highest interest rate first. I prefer this approach because **you get out of debt faster**, and it saves you the most money.

For example, you have a credit card with a $10,000 balance with a 10% interest rate and another credit card with $6,000 and a 25% interest rate. You can make $150 monthly payments on each. You might think about paying down the $10,000 debt first since it has the largest total. This will take you 98 months to pay off, and you will incur $4,657 in interest.[28] The card with the $6,000 balance will take you 87 months to pay off, and you will incur $7,034 in interest. More interest on a card that has almost half the starting balance! To get ahead of your debt payments, focus on the highest interest rate first or else the interest payments will slowly eat into your disposable income.

Balance	APR	Pay Off (Months)	Interest Paid
$10,000	10%	98	$4,657
$6,000	25%	87	$7,034

Alternatively, nothing is stopping you from adopting both methods. You could list your debts from smallest balance with the highest interest rate down to your largest balance with the lowest interest rate and go from there. I still feel this is leaving interest savings on the table, but adopt whichever approach will be more successful for you.

KEEP YOURSELF ACCOUNTABLE

Is there a good way to keep yourself accountable for paying down debts? One method is to make a promise to someone that says if you do not pay off a predetermined debt amount per month, then you will donate "insert amount" to a cause you *hate*. This is known as the commitment contract. Do this with a friend, use a website/app like Stickk,[29] something like PBwiki,[30] or even Facebook. Whichever method you use, set a predetermined goal with either money or your reputation, choose a timeline to accomplish it, and if you do not honor your commitment, follow through with the punishment.

Behavioral science tells us that we are loss-averse social animals who make decisions in a time-inconsistent manner. We hate losing things and often give in to immediate gratification, e.g., splurging, at the expense of our long-term goals, e.g., saving money. The good news is that research has discovered two factors that effectively help people achieve the behavior change they desire: Incentives and accountability.

Create a Habit

In Charles Duhigg's book *The Power of Habit*, he explains that people can change their habits if they learn how habits operate. The "habit loop" has three stages: A **cue** propels a person into a **routine** to reach the goal of a **reward**. Now, apply this to our spending habits.

In the first stage, the brain seeks a cue that will put it into automatic pilot and indicate what it should tell the body to do. The second stage is the routine, or the ensuing habit. The last stage is the reward, which teaches the brain whether the loop in question is "worth remembering for the future." When the cue and reward connect, the brain develops a strong feeling of expectation, leading to a craving and the birth of a habit. Unfortunately, the brain has difficulty determining whether the habit is a good habit or a bad habit. So, all habits are hard to break. The good news is that once you understand your cues and rewards, you can change the routine.

Change the Routine

The "golden rule of habit change" is changing the routine **but keeping the cue and reward the same**. In the context of debt repayment and saving money, determine what your cues and rewards are for spending money. For example, if you find yourself shopping to relieve stress or to feel good about yourself, determine the cause of those feelings. Are you an emotional buyer? Is it retail therapy? Does your sense of identity come from the way you dress? Is it coming from thoughts of inadequacy? Knowing what you spend your money on and why will help you understand the rewards you give yourself.

You must also know your cues. Do you shop when you had a bad day or order in when your fridge is empty? The key is to recognize these cues and create positive actions in response that replace the old routine. For example, taking a friend out for coffee when you have a bad day might replace the routine of shopping with companionship. Do not expect these habits to change overnight. Conventional wisdom says that it takes 21 days to form a new habit. Be patient and persistent when trying to create a new habit.

Start Small

Some people can go cold turkey, but for most of us, it is better to start small with changing our spending habits. Rather than saying you will only dine out once a month, try once a week. Debt repayment is the same concept. If you already have a time once a week to pay bills, that should be your cue to look over your budget and make payments on your debt. It is easiest to incorporate new routines into existing cue and reward systems. Your reward could be to enjoy a nice glass of wine and wind down for the evening. If you do not already have a set time for debt management, then you can always set a reminder to serve as your cue.

STUDENT LOAN RELIEF

Millions are struggling with student loan debt, and I was one of them. Fortunately, there are ways to get student loan relief from the government, your school, and state/province whether you live in the U.S. or Canada, if you meet certain conditions.

The Public Service Loan Forgiveness Program (U.S.)

In 2007, President George W. Bush[31] created the Public Service Loan Forgiveness (PSLF) Program that allowed student loan borrowers, who pursue government or non-profit public service jobs, to wipe out their remaining debt[32] after 10 years of on-time payments. Its purpose is to incentivize people to work in the public sector, where employees normally make less than those working in the private sector. The **public sector** is classified as working for the government or a not-for-profit organization. If you currently work in the public sector or are looking to move to the public sector and have student loans, follow these steps to qualify for the program:

1. Have the Correct Loans[33]

To qualify, you need to have a loan from the Direct program, have made all your payments in full and on time, and have worked 10 years in a public-sector service job with a qualifying employer. They are strict with the rules of qualifying for the program. First, make sure your loan is a "direct loan," which includes direct subsidized and unsubsidized loans, direct PLUS loans, and direct consolidation loans. If you have other non-qualifying loans, see if you can bundle them into a Direct Consolidation Loan. Only once your loans are under this title will your student debt payments move you along the Public Student Loan Forgiveness 10-year timeline. If you are unsure what kind of loan you have, login to your account at the Federal Student Aid site to find out.

You also need to make sure you are enrolled in the right type of repayment plan – one of the income-based programs. Double check to ensure you have a repayment plan that counts toward forgiveness. Extended repayment plans do not count.

2. Have the Correct Employer

Qualifying employers under the PSLF program include government organizations – federal, state, local, or tribal – and tax-exempt, not-for-profit organizations. You also must work full-time or more than 30 hours a week if you work for two organizations part-time. Your time with an employer does not need to be consecutive. You can work for two years in the public sector, then work in the private sector putting your 10-year timeline on pause, and then return to the public sector, continuing on the same clock.

3. Confirm You Are on Track

Each year, fill out the Employment Certification form. You will receive confirmation on the number of successful payments you have completed. However, it is important to keep records of your employment – pay stubs, taxes, anything that proves you worked at your job, just in case something goes wrong.

4. Watch for Changes in the Program

At any time, the qualifications for the program can change, so follow the latest developments at the Federal Student Loan site.

<u>Student Loan Relief from Your State or Province</u>

Some states or Canadian provinces provide niche forgiveness programs. Do your research early. You may even be eligible for a program that helps offset future education costs, such as for graduate, law, or medical school.

Student Loan Relief from Your School

Your university or college may also offer a forgiveness program. These programs, like grants, are not publicly advertised most of the time, so check with the financial aid office.

The Repayment Assistance Plan (Canada)

If you live in Canada and at least six months have passed since you graduated or left school and your loans are up to date, you may qualify for the Repayment Assistance Plan (RAP). The RAP either reduces your monthly student loan payments or removes them entirely, depending on your financial situation. If you have a permanent disability, it may also depend on your permanent disability-related expenses, which include allowable uninsured medical expenses, special care, and other expenses directly related to your disability. Enrolment is not automatic, and you must re-apply for this plan every six months.

To qualify for nullified payment requirements on your student loan, your financial situation must follow the annual gross family income thresholds by family size.

Annual Gross Family Income Thresholds for Zero Payments under RAP by Family Size

Family Size	Income Threshold
1	$25,000
2	$39,052
3	$50,457
4	$59,512
5+	$67,823

*as of 2018

If you make above these amounts, you may be eligible for a reduced monthly payment.

There are two stages to how the RAP works for a reduced monthly payment:

Stage 1

The Government of Canada and your provincial government will pay the interest owing that your revised payment does not cover. This could last up to 10 six-month periods or 60 months during the 10-year period after you leave school.

Stage 2

This stage starts once you complete Stage 1 or if you have been in repayment for over 10 years after leaving school.

During Stage 2, if you continue to have trouble meeting your repayment obligations, the government will begin to cover both the principal and interest that exceeds your reduced monthly payments. If you remain eligible for RAP, the balance of your loan is gradually paid off and the repayment obligations will not exceed 15 years, or 10 years for persons with permanent disabilities, after leaving school.

Important: If you have been approved and received a Stage 2 benefit, you cannot apply for additional student loans until your existing student loans are paid in full.

If you want to see if you qualify for the RAP, check out the online Repayment Assistance Estimator.[34]

AVOID PAYDAY LOANS

Payday loans are short-term, high-interest loans, generally for $500 or less, that are designed to bridge the gap between paychecks. They are also referred to as cash advance loans, check advance loans, deferred deposit loans, or post-dated check loans.[35] At first glance, payday loans may seem like a good idea if you are strapped for cash because whether you apply online or in-store, you are approved within minutes, and you have access almost immediately.

If you think credit cards have high interest rates, **payday loans are off the charts!** Reasons to avoid them:[36]

High Interest Rates

Loan amounts range between $50 and $1,000 depending on state laws. Fees also depend on state laws but could be structured as $15 per $100 borrowed. On the surface, that looks like a 15% interest rate, but because the loan is over such a short period, the annualized cost of borrowing is much higher. A standard payday loan with a two-week period and a $15 per $100 borrow fee has an annual rate of nearly **400%.**

Hidden Fees

For example, you receive $500 today and are required to pay back $550 in two weeks. In two weeks, you pay only the interest ($50) and rollover the loan for another two weeks. Every two weeks, you pay $50 to borrow $500. At the end of one year, you would have paid $1,300 to borrow $500, and you still owe $500. This is the payday loan trap, and it is hard to escape after falling victim to it. I call this the **downward debt death spiral**.

Moreover, the payday loan lender has direct access to your bank account, so they can withdraw the fees before you can transfer funds elsewhere to pay for rent or other bills.

Payday Loans Are Unaffordable for Most Borrowers

According to Pew Charitable Trusts,[37] 12 million Americans use payday loans every year and commonly have these characteristics:

- Likely to be renters
- Likely to earn less than $40,000 per year
- Likely to have less than a 4-year college education
- Likely to be separated or divorced

According to that same report, the average borrower takes out 8 loans of $375 for a total of $3,000 and spends $520 on interest alone by the time the initial loan is repaid.

<u>Payday Loan Alternatives</u>

- Use your emergency fund. If you save two months of salary and have springy debt, you will not be in this situation.
- Ask friends or family for a loan.
- Negotiate a payment plan with the creditor.
- Receive an advance from your employer.
- Obtain a line of credit with a much lower interest rate.
- Apply for a traditional small loan.
- Look at charitable assistance. It is not uncommon to use sites like GoFundMe where complete strangers to lend a helping hand. Alternatively, you can look to charitable organizations in your community, like the Salvation Army or United Way.

SUMMARY

Prioritize paying off your credit cards. The 15% to 25% immediate return is likely higher than any return in the stock market. In addition,

- Make more than the minimum payment per month. Even paying twice the minimum payment will allow you to pay off a credit card years faster.

- Know your credit score. Improving your credit score will allow you to obtain better rates and save you money over time. Aim to have a 700+ score.

- Conquer your debt using the 4 steps:
  1. Calculate
  2. Negotiate
  3. Consolidate
  4. Eliminate

- Use the Debt Avalanche method when eliminating your debt. Focus on the highest interest-bearing debt you have first and work down the list. The interest savings are huge.

- If you have student loans, look at the various student loan relief programs like the Public Service Loan Forgiveness Program (PSLF) in the U.S. and the Repayment Assistance Plan (RAP) in Canada. Also, see if your state or province or your university or college has a student debt relief program.

- Credit cards can be useful to build a credit score and for the rewards but only if the balance is paid in full each month. If you spend more with cards or continue to have a balance, switch to paying with cash.

- Use the commitment contract method to keep yourself accountable with a friend or online service.

- Create a habit of debt repayment by replacing the routine but keeping the cue and the reward the same.

- Stay away from store credit cards. They have higher interest rates than regular credit cards.

- Use your credit card programs. Things like warranties, car rental insurance, and trip cancellation insurance can save you a lot of money not to mention the various reward programs.

- Avoid payday loans!

CHAPTER SIX

MINIMIZE YOUR CAR EXPENSE

THE TRUE COST OF COMMUTING

I purchased my first car when I was 27. I know, I know: How could I get around without owning a car? And, what about dating? Coming out of undergrad making $40,000 a year, I could not justify it, and if a girl is only dating me because I have a car, that is not a good sign. I also had $10,000 of student loans that I needed to pay off, and it was a minimum 45-minute commute to downtown. I knew that the average person's car costs are $8,000 per year, enough to make the difference between debt and comfortable riches over time, and the fact that owning a car can be the biggest financial mistake people make. Instead, I took the bus and train, but what I should have done was move closer to work because I was not aware of the true cost of commuting.

In my scenario, driving 10 miles (16 kilometers) to work and back amounts to 20 miles a day. The government estimates the total cost of driving at $0.51 per mile, which adds up to $10.20 per day of direct driving and car ownership costs. It is possible to drive for less—likely these cheaper-to-run cars are newer, with less maintenance costs, have higher fuel efficiency, and most likely bought on credit.

At 90 minutes per day, the driving would add almost an entire work day each week. I would be like "working" 6 days a week. Flash forward 5 years, this would amount to $13,260 and 81 days spent driving.

Minutes driving=

90 minutes x 5 days x 52 weeks x 5 years= 117,000 minutes

Days driving=

117,000 / 60 minutes / 24 hours= 81.25 days

Driving cost=

$10.20 x 5 days x 52 weeks x 5 years= $13,260

In my case, it cost me $6,000 in transit passes, a difference of $7,260 that helped me achieve my savings goals. On the train, I listened to audiobooks and podcasts—over 500 hours of podcasts and 40 audio books. However, if I could do it over, and if you ever have the option, the better decision would be to move closer to work. If you take an hourly rate of $20/hour (~$40,000 a year), the true cost including the time cost would have been closer to $52,260.

Driving cost=

$10.20 x 5 days x 52 weeks x 5 years= $13,260

Hours driving=

117,000 minutes ÷ 60 minutes= 1,950 hours

Time cost=

1,950 hours x $20 an hour = $39,000

Total cost=

$39,000 + $13,260 = $52,260

Assuming you value your time at what you get paid, it is hard to justify a long commute.

REALITY CHECK ON NEW CARS

There are several popular reasons to buy a new car versus leasing or buying used:

1. New safety technology
2. Fuel efficiency
3. Low maintenance costs
4. Lower interest rates

All valid reasons. That said, I find it hard to justify buying a new car unless you are willing to own it for 10+ years and reap the benefits of no car payments in the final years of ownership. Even then, owning a used car is more appealing because you save money on car payments upfront rather than on the back end. Furthermore, if you buy a car that is three years old, for example, you still benefit from the latest safety technology and fuel efficiency without the high upfront cost. A car at that age likely will have low mileage. If you buy new, you are probably paying the car off over five to seven years. If you put that money into index funds instead of a car payment, you get a greater return. Through depreciation on new cars, you lose the most value in the first 50,000 miles, meaning this is when it is the most expensive time to own a car. Why not buy a used car with 50,000 miles already on it and invest the difference?

A new car on average:[38]

- Loses 10% of its value when you leave the lot.

- Depreciates by 15% to 25% each year over the first 5 years.

- Loses 60% of its total value over the first 5 years.

Why would you want to drive new when you can get a perfectly good used car and let someone else eat the depreciation cost?

BUY USED AND USE THE 10% RULE

If you can afford it, pay cash for a used car. When I finally made the decision, I bought a five-year-old used Honda Civic for $8,500. Cars in the $10,000 to $13,000 range are in the middle-to-upper range of the car market for most people's needs. A rule of thumb is that if you want a safe and reliable car, then only spend up to 20% of your annual income on it. If you can manage, lower is better. So, if you make $60,000, then spend a maximum of $12,000 on a car. Personally, this is too high, so I recommend the 10% rule.

<u>The 10% Rule</u>

The 10% rule means that you do not pay more than 10% of your annual salary on a car. You are likely thinking, "I don't want to drive a beater!" What about first impressions and showing off? Most people fall into this trap, which prevents them from becoming financially independent. Use this as motivation to make more money. With the 10% rule, if you earn $60,000 per year, then you are stuck driving a $6,000 car. So, think of ways to make more money. I talk about how to increase your yearly revenue in Part Two, Growth.

In all honesty, if you spend less than 20% of your gross income on a car, you are doing okay. Most people spend 50% or more. The median price of a new car is $24,000, so if you make $50,000 a year that is 48%. However, if you spend 10% or less, you are that much closer to financial independence. Even with this price restriction, you can find a reliable car that will last years, just do your research beforehand.

AVOID LEASING

Leasing a car looks like a discount compared to buying a new car, but it is terrible when compared to buying a used car. The number one reason? You do not own the vehicle. It is like paying rent on a depreciating asset. You pay the dealership the cost of the depreciation through your payments and penalties for mileage overage and wear and tear on the vehicle. Moreover, your insurance is likely higher, and if you are involved in an accident, you will have to pay the full lease amount. The benefit of owning a car outright is having zero payments and being able to put that money into investments.

WHAT IF YOU PAID TOO MUCH FOR A VEHICLE?

Everyone makes mistakes. The most important thing is being able to reflect, learn from it, and fix it. If you already bought an expensive vehicle:

1. **Keep your vehicle until it becomes 10% of your gross annual income or less**. This is the easiest solution if you have spent too much. Keep driving your car for 10+ years, and it will eventually become 10% or less of your gross annual income.

2. **Take the loss and sell your vehicle**. If you spent more than 20% of your gross income on a car, consider selling it if you are not willing to keep it until it becomes 10% of your gross annual income or less. The long-term costs of car payments, in conjunction with the lost opportunity cost of not being able to invest that cash flow, hurts you financially.

3. **Use social media to make your mistake public**. By making your mistake public, you own up to it. The last thing you want to do is admit you made the same mistake twice.

If you require a new car, look for cars that are at least three years old. Your depreciation and car insurance will be less for a used car and maintenance costs will still be low. It is also better to pay cash for a used car than finance it. Most of the 0% or low-interest offers for financing are for new cars. Used cars can have interest rates as high as 10%. That is cheaper than a credit card, but given the market, on average, rises 9.7% a year, you are falling behind.

RIDE SHARING ADVICE

When does ride sharing make sense and can you use it instead of owning a car? The answer is it depends on how often you need a car. If you need a car for your daily commute, then it is likely that owning a used car is cheaper than taking an Uber. According to the American Automobile Association (AAA), the average cost of owning and driving a sedan is **$8,876** as[39] of 2014, broken into six categories:

- Payments / depreciation: $4,260
- Fuel costs: $2,130
- Interest: $976
- Insurance: $887
- Maintenance and repairs: $355
- Registration and taxes: $355

Uber

Say you drive 5,000 miles a year. According to the U.S. Federal Highway Administration, the average commute time is 25.5 minutes, and the average number of trips per year is around 500 (keeping numbers simple). Using the rates of $1.10 per mile, $0.21 per minute, and $0.80 per trip, we calculate the following fees.

Uber base fees=

>500 trips x $0.80 per trip= $400

Mileage fees=

>5,000 miles x $1.10 per mile= $5,500

Time fees=

>500 trips x $0.21 per minute x 25.5 minutes= $2,678

Yearly Uber fees=

>$400 + $5,500 + $2,678= $8,578

Monthly Uber fees=

>$8,578 / 12 months= $714.83

Based on AAA's average yearly cost of $8,876, using Uber at a cost of **$8,578** a year is a better choice if you drive less than 5,000 miles per year.

Zipcar

An alternative to Uber is Zipcar's Commuter Service where you receive a Zipcar from 5:00 am Monday to 7:00 pm Friday for a $249 monthly fee plus $0.45 per mile for the miles you drive. Parking, gas, and insurance are included in the membership. If you drive 5,000 miles per year, this equates to $2,250 for the miles driven plus $2,988 for the monthly fees over the course of the year for a total cost of **$5,238.** This cost is much cheaper than Uber for the same distance. In fact, your commute needs to be 13,000 miles per year to match what the average cost of owning and driving a sedan is. Not a bad deal. The only caveat is the service is only in selected cities and does not include driving on the weekends.

Zipcar Commuter yearly fee (5,000 miles)=
   ($249 x 12) + (5,000 miles x $0.45)= $5,238

Zipcar Commuter yearly fee (13,000 miles)=
   ($249 x 12) + (13,000 miles x $0.45)= $8,838

MONEY-SAVING TIPS

Most people do not realize that taking on a car payment is one of the worst things to do when trying to create wealth. The car payment is the largest cost after home mortgage/rent, so it eats up more income than pretty much anything else. The average car payment is $495 a month over 64 months, and once they pay off their car, most people take on another payment because the allure of having a new car is too much! Get out of this cycle and invest that money instead. Over 40 years, $5,940 a year saved becomes **$2,658,575!**[40]

If you need a car, follow these rules:

1. **Never Borrow Money to Buy a Car**

Smart, frugal people do not buy new cars, and they never buy on credit.

2. **Buy a Car That Does Whatever You Need It for Most**

Your default vehicle should be a car unless you use a truck for work, SUV for off-road excursions, or another vehicle where a car is inappropriate. Otherwise, the "what-if" scenarios of buying a different vehicle will cost you more money than it is worth for the few times you might use it.

3. **Limit Your Driving**

Many people believe if they are making payments on their cars, then they may as well use the car as much as possible since it only costs them their monthly payment. This is the wrong mentality.

The more you drive your car, the faster it will wear out—tires, maintenance, gas, it all adds up. This is another reason why it is better to live close to work.

SAVE ON CAR INSURANCE

Shop around for car insurance. Get at least three price quotes and have insurers compete for your business. Ask friends and relatives for their recommendations. Also, look at insurance costs *before* you purchase a car. The last thing you want is an unplanned cost. When searching car insurance, keep these factors in mind:

- Do not shop by price alone. Look at other variables such as fuel economy, mileage, and what condition the car is in.
- Ask for higher deductibles, which can reduce your collision and comprehensive coverage by 15% to 30%. Have enough spare cash in your emergency fund to pay in case you have a claim.
- Buy your homeowners and auto insurance from the same insurer. Many companies give you a break if you buy two or more types of insurance from them. You may also receive a reduction if you insure more than one vehicle with them.
- Some companies offer reductions to drivers who obtain insurance through a group plan. So if possible, use your employer; professional, business, and alumni groups; or other associations.

SUMMARY

Remember, owning a car is one of the worst things to do when trying to create wealth. Ask yourself if you require a car or if it is a nice to have. Can you get by using other means?

- If you have a lengthy commute, move closer to your work. Less travel means you will be happier on average and save money on wear and tear on your car, gas, and your personal time.

- Buy used. Try to keep the cost under 20% of your annual salary, preferably 10%.

- Avoid leases.

- Try not to borrow money to buy a car.

- Determine if ride sharing is an option if you do not need daily transportation.

- Limit your driving to make your car last longer.

- Shop around for car insurance for the best deal.

CHAPTER SEVEN

HAVE INSURANCE JUST IN CASE

RECOMMENDED CRITERIA

I hate paying for insurance. I think to myself, "Why am I paying a premium for a 'what if?' scenario?" Some argue that insurance of all types—car, house, health, life—is a big waste of money. And in some cases, insurance is bought partly out of fear and without any consideration to whether it is a good deal. If you are an average consumer, you are likely spending thousands of dollars per year on various insurance. Is it a waste of money? Not if you are getting insurance for these reasons:

1. You are forced to have insurance, e.g., a bank requiring car or house insurance.

2. You cannot afford not to have insurance if something goes awry, e.g., with your health or if your house were to burn down.

3. You are riskier than the insurance company thinks you are, e.g., you drag race your car on the weekends or know you might be diagnosed with or are currently have an existing health condition.

All other insurance is arguably a waste of money. Extended warranties? Forget about it. Identity theft insurance? Credit card balance protection insurance? No way. Take the money you would have used to purchase those policies and put it into an index fund ETF, which I discuss in Chapter 10: Invest in the Index. Insurance companies know the odds are in their favor. Otherwise, they would be out of business.

When you buy insurance, it better be for the right reason. An accident or disaster could leave you in financial ruin in an instant. Do your research and avoid overpaying when you look for a policy.

1. Only Insure Against Things That Can Ruin You Financially

- Your house or rental unit
- Your car
- Traveling overseas and becoming sick
- Going to the hospital
- Death or permanent disability
- Being unable to work

2. Have High Deductibles to Save on Premiums

3. Negotiate Your Insurance Premiums Every Year

Many different insurance types and products exist. How do you know what you need coverage on and how much? It can be overwhelming, not to mention the high-pressure sales tactics that you may face when looking for a policy. As a general guideline, I recommend homeowner's / renter's insurance, car insurance, life insurance, disability insurance, health insurance, and travel insurance at a minimum. However, other types of insurance may also be essential, depending on your situation.

RENTER'S AND HOMEOWNER'S INSURANCE

A home is often our largest asset, so insuring it is essential to protect our net worth from unexpected disasters. Homeowner's insurance covers the cost of rebuilding or making repairs to your home if it is damaged or destroyed by a disaster like a tornado or fire. It also covers the contents of your home up to a fixed dollar amount.

Renter's insurance is just as important as homeowner's insurance. Most renters do not realize that the landlord's insurance will not typically cover personal property when damaged or destroyed. And, this policy is affordable, often cheaper than homeowner's insurance.

Both policies offer some protection inside and outside of your home. If someone slips and breaks their leg on your property or your dog bites someone, your policy could cover the medical bills. And, coverage usually insures your belongings when you travel as well as offering financial protection from theft.

In most cases, flood insurance is not included in either policy. If you live in a flood-prone zone, I highly recommend buying a separate flood insurance policy.

Keep receipts and photos of everything for your records. Use the app of your insurer, if they have one, or a website like Sortly to keep a copy of your inventory online. Apps like Evernote, Google Keep, and Microsoft's OneNote are also an option as they allow you to take a picture of an object, tag it, and store it.

Read the fine print of your insurance policy, too. Some insurers have a bad reputation of denying coverage for technicalities like only protecting against rising waters and not burst pipes. Read reviews online, check *Consumer Reports*, and do your research.

CAR INSURANCE

With car insurance, you want to protect yourself against collision and liability. In no-fault states in the U.S., you also need medical payments coverage.

Collision protects your car, and the level of coverage depends on the car you are driving. Insurance companies only reimburse you for the book value of your car, so if you are driving a $2,000 beater, then it might be worth driving without collision. Otherwise, I recommend full coverage for collision.

Liability insurance is the critical part of car insurance. Whatever you do, do *not* sign up for the minimum coverage. Liability pays the bills if anyone is injured in a car accident. If you do not have adequate coverage, your financial future could be in jeopardy. I suggest full coverage for liability.

No-fault states require drivers to pay for their own costs after a car accident, regardless of who is at fault. This insurance is known as medical payments coverage, personal injury protection, or no-fault insurance.

With any insurance, choose higher deductibles to save on premiums, but ensure that you have the cash on hand to cover the deductible if the unfortunate occurs. Consider buying all your insurance from the same provider if they offer a discount.

LIFE INSURANCE

There is some debate about whether to purchase life insurance when you are single or only when you have children. The argument for having life insurance when you are single is to have money to pay for your own funeral costs or if you are financially responsible for another person. Additionally, the younger you are, the cheaper the insurance premiums.

If you have kids or have anyone financially dependent upon you, then life insurance is usually a necessity. Through your work or as an individual, have life insurance equal to about 10 times your income, more than that if you have several young children. You want your income replaced if something happens to you. If something happens to you when your kids are young, then that can be a lot of money. I recommend the following when choosing insurance coverage:

Buy Term Life Insurance

Term life insurance is typically the cheapest life insurance. It offers protection for a set time, usually between 1 and 30 years. You typically pay an annual fee and are covered for another year. Think of it as paying for peace of mind that you are covered in case something happens. I recommend a policy that keeps the same price each year. This is called level term and prevents your annual premium from unexpectedly increasing. I further recommend a 30-year level term insurance policy even if you think you may not need it. You can cancel anytime.

Shop Around and Avoid Universal Life Insurance

Shop around when looking for insurance policies. Each insurance company will have different rates, so search for the best quote. Compare them online.

Also, be careful because insurance salesmen typically lead you away from term insurance and try to sell you whole life insurance, also called universal life insurance or a cash value policy. These policies try to sell you on the idea of paying for coverage and a little extra to be invested in the stock market. The insurance salesman receives higher commissions on selling these policies.

What they do not tell you is the rates of return can change and may not be as attractive later down the road. Why not buy term insurance, which has lower premiums, and invest the difference in ETFs yourself? The investment options are limited and will not be in low-cost index funds. And, if you want to cancel your coverage and take out your cash, you could find yourself on the hook for surrender charges.

LONG-TERM DISABILITY

Your most powerful financial asset is neither your home nor your car. It is your ability to make money! If you have children, you need disability insurance. For many young people, having disability insurance is more important than life insurance. Statistically if you are 32 or older, you are about 12 times more likely to become disabled than to die by the age of 65. Again, check to see if you have this option through work. Otherwise, purchase it on your own. You can usually find coverage that is between 50% and 70% of your income.

HEALTH INSURANCE

You need health insurance. Period. Fortunately, in Canada, we are covered. In the United States, however, the number one cause of bankruptcy today is medical bills. The Affordable Care Act (ACA), otherwise known as Obamacare, allows everyone access to insurance, which helps. Insurance companies can no longer turn you down for a pre-existing condition. Having health insurance should arguably be your number one priority. The last thing you want is to bankrupt yourself and your family because you did not have health insurance.

As with any insurance policies, do your homework. If you do not have access through your work, get health insurance through a state health insurance marketplace or obtain it on your own. Check out HealthCare.gov and eHealth.com for rates. Also, see if you can be covered through a family member. Federal rules say your parents can cover you until the age of 26, and some states allow even longer.

One way to control costs is to have large deductibles to lower your premium. Consider opening a Health Savings Account (HSA), which allows you to save for medical expenses in a tax-free savings account. If you end up not using the money in your HSA when you are working, do not worry. It grows tax-free and can be used to pay for medical expenses in retirement.

Be warned, however, that most policies still require you to pay out-of-pocket expenses, even if you have coverage. The Affordable Care Act only allows you to purchase coverage during specific enrolment periods, so get coverage during that time.

DENTAL INSURANCE

According to the National Association of Dental Plans, 74 million Americans, about 1 in 4, had no dental coverage in 2016. To put things into perspective: The uninsured dental rate has increased to four times the medically uninsured rate. This is dangerous to a person's financial well-being, considering how expensive dental work can be and the side effects of not regularly receiving dental care. Statistics show that those without dental benefits report higher incidences of other illness:

- 67% are more likely to have heart disease

- 50% are more likely to have osteoporosis

- 29% are more likely to have diabetes

They also visit the dentist less frequently, missing opportunities for prompt treatment and prevention. Over two million visits to the emergency room are for dental treatment annually.

According to the ADA Health Policy Institute's 2013 Survey of Dental Fees, which is the latest data available, average costs in the U.S. for common dental procedures:[41]

- Teeth cleaning adult: $85

- White dental filling (one surface, anterior): $149

- Silver filling: $125

- Porcelain crown fused to noble metal: $1,003

- Complete series of intra-oral X-rays: $124

Dental services are not cheap. Chances are you have a plan at work. If you not, consider a discount network, like DentalPlans.com, where you can receive a 15% to 50% discount on service and treatments from participating dentists for $100 to $200 a year. Or, use a service like Brighter.com to compare dental rates and the reputation of dentists in your area. In Canada, look at discount services like ClubDental.ca. Ensure that the discounts you receive are enough to cover the annual fee. Otherwise, it is not worth it. Also, carefully read the limits and restrictions.

Why not buy individual coverage if you are not covered at work? Unfortunately, most plans have poor coverage.[42] Dental insurance premiums can also be more expensive than simply paying out of your pocket for routine checkups and cleanings. The reason is that people are more likely to use their dental benefits, increasing the premiums for everyone. The cost for individual coverage is about $350 a year for a typical individual policy compared to $19 to $32 a month, or $228 to $384 a year, through employee and group policies.

Another disadvantage to individual plans is the waiting period, which typically does not apply to group plans. For example, most individual plans do not cover fillings for the first six months of a policy and may not offer coverage for other procedures for up to 18 months. This prevents people from signing up for an insurance policy, having the work done, and then dropping the insurance coverage right after. If you are not covered at work, the discount network is the way to go.

LONG-TERM CARE INSURANCE

If you are under the age of 60, this insurance is not for you. If you are over 60, buy long-term care insurance to cover in-care or nursing home care. Otherwise, the average nursing home is between $40,000 and $70,000 a year. Something most people do not plan for when saving for retirement.

TRAVEL INSURANCE

Travel insurance sounds like buying an overpriced extended warranty, but you should purchase it every time you travel abroad, even if your credit card already offers coverage. Your credit card often has limitations on the amount of coverage and the amount of time you are covered. You can also be denied coverage based on your age and medical history. Moreover, the primary benefit of having travel insurance is for the medical emergency and evacuation coverage, which credit cards can have limitations on.

However, if you decide to stick with your credit card coverage, check to see if you are covered for the duration of your trip. You can often extend coverage for an additional fee. Also, see if you qualify since cards with travel insurance exclude you if you fall outside their policies parameters. The one exception to requiring additional travel insurance is if you have a policy through benefits with your work. In that case, a combined credit card and work coverage should provide enough to be safe.

There are 5 types of coverage to look for when shopping for travel insurance:

1. Medical Emergencies and Evacuation

This is the number one reason for travel insurance. A few years ago when I was visiting Tokyo, I had a case of strep throat. Being in a foreign country with a language barrier, I did not know what to do at first but did not want my sore throat and fever to ruin my vacation. Fortunately, I had travel insurance. I called the number on the policy, and they referred me to a nearby clinic. $350 and 30 minutes later, I was in and out with my antibiotics. The policy only cost me $60, so I was ahead financially. Imagine if I had suffered something more severe because the costs can add up quickly!

For more severe emergencies, hospital costs can approach $50,000 per day in some parts of the world, and medical transport home can exceed $100,000. Read the fine print on the policy for the limits on coverage for emergency evacuation, medical expenses, and emergency dental work. Purchase the coverage you are comfortable with. Some credit cards offer emergency and evacuation coverage, but they have limitations, so read the fine print. For example, my credit card[43] offers coverage for trips for up to 15 consecutive days if I am under the age of 65. If I am over the age of 65, I am only covered for 3 consecutive days. Furthermore, it does not cover pre-existing medical conditions. It is always better to have extra coverage, just in case.

2. Trip Cancellation and Interruption

This covers costs if you suddenly cannot go on your trip for reasons such as an illness, accident, or death of a close relative. In the unfortunate event that you must cancel a scheduled trip or cut the trip short, your credit card may not cover all your losses.

Note: Trip cancellation and interruption insurance generally only covers the portion of your trip that you buy before you leave. If you are already on your trip and buy the rest of your tickets when abroad, you are out of luck.

3. Baggage and Personal Belongings

While most people buy travel insurance to protect the loss of their belongings, this is arguably the least important aspect of travel insurance. Your health is the most important and potentially the costliest when traveling abroad without insurance. However, it is nice to have your personal items covered in case of theft. You do not want to have to replace a $1,000 laptop or camera if it is stolen. If your credit card offers coverage, research the limitations.

My card's coverage is limited to burglary in a hotel with visible signs of forceful entry, up to a maximum coverage of $2,500. If pickpocketed, I am out of luck.

There are, however, serious exclusions. Most of the time, insurance only covers losses with a police report, which makes sense. But a police report can be difficult to obtain in some countries. On top of that, most policies will not cover unattended belongings. If you went for a swim with your phone on your towel and it was stolen, then you are not covered.

Pro-tip: If you have homeowner's or renter's insurance, then your belongings may be covered on your trip. Usually, there is a limit of around 10% of the total coverage on your policy, and your deductible applies to any claims while traveling.

4. Accidental Death or Dismemberment Insurance

If you or your loved one dies on a trip or suffers a life-impairing accident, like losing a hand, this covers you.

5. Personal Liability

If you are in an accident or accidentally cause damage, then this coverage will be applied to your liability and legal expenses. Do not confuse this with car insurance, and not all travel insurance policies cover this.

Remember to purchase travel insurance before your trip, not during or after, otherwise the coverage is void.

For Canadians: If you are away more than six months, obtain a written extension from your provincial health care plan if you live in a province that allows you to do so. If you are traveling within Canada, each province operates differently regarding how your provincial health care plan works when in another province. Some provinces cover physicians but exclude chiropractors and prescription drugs. Others make you pay out of pocket and then reimburse you. Quebec operates differently and does not direct bill at all and only covers certain services.

Travel Insurance Quote Checklist

When looking for a travel insurance quote, ask these questions:

- What is the amount of liability covered?
- Is trip cancellation or trip interruption insurance included?
- Is there a refund available for the unused amount?
- What is the deductible?
- Do you offer a medical service assistance, meaning can you help me find a doctor or hospital?
- Is the policy valid worldwide, including my home country?
- Can I buy my initial insurance after I leave on my trip?
- Can I add to my insurance after I leave on my trip?

SUMMARY

The goal of insurance is to protect your net worth from unexpected life events. Remember the following:

- The 3 reasons to have insurance:

    1. You are forced to have insurance.

    2. You cannot afford not to have insurance.

    3. You are riskier than the insurance company thinks.

- As a general guideline, have coverage for car insurance with liability as a minimum, homeowner's / renter's insurance, health insurance, disability insurance, and long-term care insurance, if you are over the age of 60. Strongly consider travel insurance when traveling abroad.

- Raise deductibles to save on premiums. Negotiate your premiums every year to save money, and shop around for insurance rates using online quotes to find the best prices.

- If you have dependents, get term life insurance.

- If you are not covered for dental benefits by your work, look at discount networks to save.

PART TWO

GROWTH

The most important asset you have is yourself. If you have a full-time job, focus first on being a superstar there. Work as hard and efficiently as possible. Get more done than anyone else, be noticed, and work toward earning a promotion and raise. An investment in your career is the biggest payoff you can make. Chapter 8: Negotiate Salaries & Raises focuses on how to make more at your 9-to-5 job by negotiating for a higher starting salary and increasing your income through raises.

The second part of the equation to earning more money is starting a side hustle. I believe everyone should have a side hustle to increase your earning potential, but do not neglect your full-time job to do it.

Studies show that entrepreneurs who start a business while still employed tend to do better than those who do not. Blowing through your savings is not an attractive prospect if you decide to jump full-time into your side hustle too soon. In Chapter 9: Have a Side Hustle, you learn how to come up with side hustle ideas and tips on getting started.

CHAPTER EIGHT

NEGOTIATE SALARIES & RAISES

SALARIES

Negotiating your salary[44] when starting a new job and negotiating a raise at your current position are two great ways to increase your income.

I will be the first to admit I did not negotiate my salary for my first job out of university. Graduating in 2010 and coming out of the 2008-2009 Financial Crisis, I told myself I was lucky to even have a position in finance, even if it only paid $40,000 per year. In retrospect, it was a mistake. Fortunately, I learned quickly, and for my second job, when the company came back with an offer I was not happy with, I negotiated a $15,000 increase over my previous salary.

Everyone should negotiate their pay when starting a new job. You can easily make $5,000 to $10,000 more per year by negotiating. This increase can add up to over $300,000 over a career. Invested properly into index funds, assuming a 25% tax rate, you are looking at between $639,403 (with a $5,000 increase) and $1,278,806 (with a $10,000 increase) over 30 years. You must negotiate. Every dollar counts.

Do Your Homework

Before you go into the interview, have a minimum salary in mind. Base this on careful research using tools like Salary.com, PayScale.com, and GlassDoor.com. Quiz people you know in the industry on what the position is likely to pay. Research, however, is often not enough. You must sell yourself during the interview. Focus on the value you bring to the company not what comparable salaries are. Negotiate for more than just money. Job titles, bonuses, stock options, and vacation days are all benefits in the total compensation package.

Postpone Salary Negotiations Until the Job Is Offered

It is important that salary negotiations should only occur once you have a job offer. Talking compensation too early, especially if you are initiating the discussion, shows you only care about money, and you will likely be cut from the interview process. If the potential employer is asking you about your salary expectations, avoid giving a number.

Let the Other Side Make the First Offer

If asked what your salary expectations are before the job offer, say that you want to know more about the responsibilities and challenges of the role before discussing pay. You do not want to price yourself out of the job. If you discuss compensation early in the interview process, you have not yet demonstrated enough value to the employer. And, they could put a red flag on your application that you are expecting too much. Salary talks should happen at the end of the offer process after you have had a chance to prove your value, meaning when they do not want to lose you.

How to Negotiate Your Salary

Noel Smith-Wenkle was a job headhunter in the 1980s and developed the following method, which has proven successful for salary negotiations.[45] In practice, his technique involves 4 steps:

1. If the company asks for a number on the application, leave it blank.

2. When the company verbally asks how much you will take, say, "I'm much more interested in doing [type of work] at [name of company] than I am in the size of the

initial offer." Smith-Wenkle says this will suffice about 40% of the time.

3. If the company asks a second time, your answer should be, "I will consider any reasonable offer." Smith-Wenkle says this polite stalling tactic will work another 30% of the time.

4. About 30% of the time, you will reach this final step. Again, your response will be a polite refusal to answer the question, "You're in a much better position to know how much I'm worth to you than I am." This is your final answer, no matter how many times the company tries to get you to go first.

The purpose of this method is to make the company name a number first. Once the company makes an offer, repeat the number, and then stop talking. Jack Chapman in his book *Negotiating Your Salary: How to Make $1,000 a Minute* calls this "the flinch." "The most likely outcome of this silence is a raise," he says. This technique will buy you time while putting pressure on the employer. Often, they will come back with a higher offer thinking that they gave too low of a salary. Using silence is more effective than tears, anger, or aggression. Silence is golden.

Counter with a Researched Response

Base your counteroffer on what you know about yourself, the value you can bring to the company, the market, and what competitors pay. It is crucial to do your research beforehand. Tie your work to the company's strategic goals, and show how you will make the manager look good. If you are just out of school and do not have much work experience, focus on your strong work ethic and positive attitude. Ask for at least 10% more than what the offer is and see what they say.

Be persistent. In many cases, the employer will reject your first request for a higher offer. Gently push back, justifying your reasoning again. It is essential to show the value you are providing the company, whether your work experience can save them time or make them money. Without demonstrating how you can achieve either, it is unlikely they will raise their offer.

Have a Second Job Offer

Another technique is to have a second job offer. When an employer knows that they have competition for you, it increases your value. So, interview at multiple places at the same time. In addition, see which company you would be happier at because money is not everything. Do not say the name of the company you have the second offer from. You do not want any side channel conversations between the firms.

Accepting the Offer

Once a company makes an offer, you have two options. If the offer is above your minimum salary expectations, take the job, assuming the complete compensation package is satisfactory. If it is below your minimum, tell them it is too low, but do not say by how much. Consider more than just the salary if your employer offers the following:

- Health insurance
- Life / Disability insurance
- Matching retirement contributions
- Vacation days

Be flexible, too. If the company will not budge on salary, negotiate other perks. Ask for things like an extra week of vacation, a different title, a private office, or a flexible schedule. If they say no at this point, it is acceptable to stop negotiating. You do not want to seem greedy and create bad will.

RAISES

Your career is your biggest financial asset. If you take your annual salary, say you start at $50,000 per year, and earn 3% average annual pay increases, you will make $4.6 million over a 45-year career. And, it does not take much additional earnings to make a huge difference. Landing 4% raises instead of 3% earns you almost $1.4 million more. If you think you deserve a raise, try these approaches:

<u>Ensure Your Performance Deserves a Raise Before You Ask</u>

If you are going to negotiate for an increase in salary, you must show that you deserve it. So, keep track of your worth to the company by monitoring what you do over time. One of the biggest mistakes in a job is not having proof that you are indispensable. If you know your performance is average or sub-par, do not ask for a raise. However, if you have been showing up to work on time, putting in 110%, and going above and beyond your job description, you will have more leverage when you ask.

<u>It Is Not You vs. Them</u>

Sometimes, it is easy to fall into the trap of thinking that negotiation is a zero-sum game—for you to win, the company must lose and vice versa. Changing this mindset is crucial to improving your chances for a successful outcome. Instead, view the negotiation as a discussion and partnership. Focus on your successes, what you have been doing, and what you will continue to do for the company.

Do Your Homework

The first rule when asking for a raise is knowing what your job pays. Look online to see if you are underpaid for your position using websites like Salary.com, PayScale.com, and GlassDoor.com. LinkedIn is another excellent resource.

Do Not Compare Yourself to Colleagues

If, during your research, you find out a colleague is making more than you for the same position, never mention them by name when asking for a raise. It makes you look petty, and perhaps there are legitimate reasons why your colleague is making more than you. Alternatively, focus on the value you bring to the firm.

Timing Is Everything

When it comes to asking for a raise, timing is everything. Wait until you and/or the business share a success before approaching your supervisor. Maybe you just completed a large project or initiative for the company or attracted new business. Whatever it may be, make sure your success is still fresh in your manager's mind.

Another good time to talk about a raise is during your performance review, if you receive a good assessment. It would naturally lead to compensation talks, assuming you did your homework and concluded that based on market data you are worth a raise.

If your employer says no, do not get angry. Keep in mind you are not entitled to a raise. The last thing you want to do is create animosity by using hardball tactics with a raise negotiation. Gently push back by focusing on the value your accomplishments have created for the firm or switch to asking about other benefits like professional development opportunities.

If they still say no, ask what else you can do in the future to show your worth. This is a natural way to bring up negotiations again at a future date when you can prove to them you did as suggested.

Practice

Practice what you are going to say with a friend or in front of a mirror. This will ease your nerves and boost your confidence. Another suggestion is to negotiate in real-world scenarios, such as with your insurance company, internet provider, or credit card company, to gain valuable experience.

Do Not Name a Number

Just like with salary negotiations, do your research ahead of time and do not name a number. The question will likely pop up. Say that you would be happy with a number they think you deserve. If they come back with a number that is not satisfactory, you now know you have some wiggle room to negotiate higher. Be willing to compromise. For example, if they come back with a 3% raise, ask for 5%, and you may settle at 4%.

Consider More Than Money

Sometimes, your company may not be able to give you a raise. So, you may find that asking for non-monetary perks or extended benefits ends up being more valuable to you and your lifestyle. Professional development opportunities, a flexible work environment, fitness memberships, vacation days, or whatever you value beyond money makes excellent compensation.

SUMMARY

Your career is your number one financial asset. So, negotiating your salary when receiving a job offer and negotiating raises with your current job are great ways to achieve your financial goals. Remember the following:

- Do your research on what the position pays, whether through online websites, like GlassDoor.com or PayScale.com, or through colleagues at the company where you are interviewing. This is critical.

- Wait until you receive a job offer before negotiating your salary. Bringing up salary talks too early in the interview process can have a negative effect on your ability to receive an offer.

- Always focus on the value you can bring the firm when negotiating an offer, or if you are negotiating a raise, on the value you have brought and will continue to bring.

- Negotiate for things other than salary if the company is not willing to increase their offer. Vacation days, titles, and other benefits are possibilities.

- Always have the employer be the first to mention a number, and negotiate from there.

- With raise negotiations, timing is everything. Wait until your annual review or when you and/or the company has had recent success. You must prove that you performed more than your job description or else you risk creating bad will with your company.

- Practice. Doing a mock negotiation with a friend or parent is a good step.

CHAPTER NINE

HAVE A SIDE HUSTLE

ANYONE CAN MAKE EXTRA INCOME

A limit exists on how much you can save, but there is no limit to how much you can earn. If you want to retire faster, increase your income while saving more. If you make an extra $100 a month and invest it in index funds, it will be worth over $200,000 in 30 years. I believe everyone should have a side income. Even if you love your job, having multiple sources of income reduces the burden of having to earn everything with your day job. In Chris Guillebeau's book *Side Hustle*, he describes steps to bringing in side income in less than a month, while requiring less than an hour a day. The best part? You do not need a business degree to do it.

My first experience having a side hustle was in 1996. I was sipping hot chocolate while waiting for my younger brother to finish his hockey game when an idea occurred to me. If people were willing to buy hot chocolate for $3 at the rink, would they be ready to purchase hot chocolate from an 11-year-old boy? Suddenly, ideas of video games and wandering down the toy aisle filled my head. I pitched the idea to my mom, and after some thought, I decided to go for it.

At the next hockey game, I set up shop outside the rink, selling hot chocolate before and after the event for $1 a cup. As an extra incentive, I hand drew comics from a comic book I was reading at the time for the adults to have a chuckle. Let me tell you, handing over those cups of hot chocolate felt like grueling work during those early mornings outside in the bitter cold. Finally, with the hockey game over, and everyone on their way home, I peeked into my jar and knew I could afford another Super Nintendo game.

This opened an entirely new world of possibilities to earn extra income and a lesson I continue to apply to this day.

Years later at Toys "R" Us, I found a sale on a video game. When I looked up the price on eBay, I found that I could make a lot of money. So, I bought all the copies and proceeded to convince every electronics store in the city to price match them. All in all, I bought 50 copies of the game, making over $20 per game after reselling them.

Another example was a night in November 2006. I camped outside Walmart for 8 hours waiting for the release of the PlayStation 3 to resell it and make a $400 profit. $50 per hour, not bad I told myself as I was shivering in the cold, making small talk with the other overnighters.

The most extreme example of my eBay side hustle was back in university during the launch of the iPhone 4. I called every store in the city multiple times per day to see when the next shipment would arrive. If they had any in stock, I dropped everything I was doing to buy as many as I could. Each phone made me $250 profit, and I managed to snag 20 of them before supply caught up with demand. Ultimately, I paid for my semester's tuition with that gig.

Guillebeau explains in his book that the secret to having a side hustle is not having classroom knowledge, but going out there and doing. Real-world knowledge is far more applicable than what you can find in a textbook. His book helps break down the complete process of planning and action, condensed into a 27-day timeline.

Guillebeau says you first want to create goals for yourself when you start a side hustle. Three common objectives are:

1. Make extra cash for a specific purpose, like paying off a loan, saving up for a big-ticket item, taking a vacation, or building up your emergency fund.

2. Create a sustainable and ongoing source of income that makes a difference in your quality of life.

3. Replace or exceed the income from your current job.

No one goal is better than the next. It depends on your individual circumstances, and these can change over time. I recommend investing at least a portion of what you make with your side hustle in index funds, which I discuss in detail in Chapter 10: Invest in the Index. If you can invest it all, then even better.

Feasible, Profitable, Appealable

Finding an idea that works is not always easy. When starting a side income, some ideas are better than others. The three criteria to use are: Feasibility, profitability, and appealability.

Feasibility: A feasible idea is one that you can start *right now* using the skills, time, and resources you already have. The more viable the idea, the better chances you can act on it right now without overthinking it.

Profitability: Your idea must have the potential to make money. If it is too elaborate, it will require too much work and effort to get it off the ground. A quick test is to see if you can describe the concept in a sentence or two. If not, then it will require too much work to be profitable.

Appealability: If you were a customer of your product or service would you buy it? Would your friends purchase it if they were not your friends? This is key to any idea that can make money.

Focus on High-Potential Ideas

Ideas that are not good right away usually have the following characteristics:

- The idea is too involved, meaning it will take too much time and effort to set up.
- The idea is something you have no idea how to make or do not currently have the skills to make it happen.
- The idea is too vague.
- The idea is something that takes a lot of time to produce or takes a lot of your time to maintain.

Ideas that have potential usually have the following characteristics:

- Simple and easy to execute.
- Easily describable in one sentence.
- Solves a problem or improves someone's life, and they are willing to spend money on it. If it solves a problem you have, all the better. Tim Ferriss calls this scratching your own itch.
- Does not take a lot of time to maintain.
- Will bring in money continuously.

How do you come up with ideas?

CREATE A LIST OF IDEAS

Side hustle opportunities are all around you. Narrowing down the options is not be about what gig you should do but what you do not want to do. If you are going to be doing something on the side, it may as well be something you enjoy. The first step then is to create a list of ideas, both yours and borrowed.

When coming up with ideas, keep in mind that you are not looking for a part-time job. You are looking for something that makes your life easier while making you money. Ask yourself what do people need or want? This is referred to as creating value. Value is created when someone makes something useful and shares it with the world. When thinking of ideas, focus on scratching your own itch. What hobbies, skills, or passions can you make money with? Find a market, define your customers, and develop a product or service for them. Solving your own need is a great way to start. Chances are other people will have the same need and pay money for it. Ideas usually fall under one of three categories:

1. Products
2. Services
3. Being a middleman

Come up with 3 qualified ideas and ask yourself these questions about each:

- What do you need to get started, and what are the costs involved? Your idea becomes more realistic if you can jot down your requirements and focus on your priorities one at a time.

- What are the potential barriers to you starting your idea? Is it fear or money?

- Has anyone done this before? If so, how can you make your idea different or better? The main benefit should be explainable in one sentence or phrase. Most ideas have been done before. It all comes down to how you execute, which leads back to how do you make your idea better or different.

- What is the best-case scenario? This is hard to quantify. We all want to make millions of dollars, but keep this goal realistic. It is important that the success of your idea is not dependent on how much money you make but what you learn along the way. Your first side hustle could be a total failure, but if you learn something useful, you can apply it to a future endeavor.

- What is the worst-case scenario? You want to cap your downside risk by starting small. Whether your budget is $100 or $1,000, pick a number that you are comfortable risking.

MAKING MONEY WITH PRODUCTS

When creating an income using products, do it using one of the following ways according to Tim Ferriss in the *4-Hour Workweek*:

Option 1: Resell a Product

This is the easiest way to sell a product but also the least profitable due to the lack of differentiation and competition among other retailers. To get started, you usually contact the manufacturer and request a wholesale price list, generally 40% off retail, and terms. Then, you try to sell the product, either at your own brick-and-mortar location or set up your own online store.

Option 2: License a Product

This is the most complicated way to sell. As a licensor, you can create a product, and then license it out to others to manufacture, collecting a paycheck for every item sold. Typically, you make 10% of the wholesale price, with the rest being kept by the licensee.

The other way is to be the licensee, allowing you to create and sell the product. The licensee keeps most of the profit, but the role requires a lot of negotiating and legal work. Which leads us to the third option, which is the least complicated and most profitable.

Option 3: Create a Product

There are three ways to do this:
1. Create the content yourself, using a variety of sources and mixing and matching them to create a unique product.

2. Repurpose information that is in the public domain that is not subject to copyright law.

3. License content or hire an expert to help create the content.

#1 and #2 require you to be an "expert" on the subject matter you are catering to. Being an expert does not mean you need to know everything. It means you must know more than 80% of what the general public knows on a subject. If you have a passion, then you are already there. Add a little more research, and you can easily create a product based on your knowledge.

An alternative to knowledge-based products is to start a drop shipping business. It allows you to sell a product directly to the customer without having to buy any inventory. You do not invest money in purchasing products, keeping your risk low. The manufacturer not only carries the stock, but they also ship it directly to the customer for you. Your main focus is marketing and customer service. With drop shipping, you can start a business with any of your favorite passions. Almost any niche can be sold using this method. You can either create your own product (recommended), outsourcing production and inventory management, or resell an existing product.

Pricing Products

If you decide to create a product, the product should cost between $50 and $200. Pricing low is shortsighted because you want to provide value to your customers, and often it can be difficult to provide value if the product is priced low. Moreover, focusing on price alone can lead to a race to the bottom mentality. Many companies are switching to upmarket products in search of growth. Some examples are Starbucks, who charge as much as $12 a cup in response to specialty roasters, and movie theaters, who offer a more premium experience to compete with Netflix. Besides giving people more value, look at three more reasons why you should price your product high:

1. Higher pricing means you can sell more units with less work. It often takes just as much work to sell a lower-priced product as it does a higher-priced product.

2. Higher pricing attracts low-maintenance customers, which can save you time.

3. Higher pricing usually means higher profit margins.

Tim Ferriss recommends pricing your product with an 8x to 10x markup, which means if the product costs $10 to make, then aim to sell it between $80 and $100. If you go the retail route, by the time wholesalers and retailers take their cut, you still want enough left over to make it worth your time. The exception to this markup rule is if your product is information, like selling a guide or a how-to tutorial. It did not cost you anything to make other than the initial time investment, so your markup is exponentially higher. An additional benefit of selling information-based products is that it takes a lot more effort for others to copy your idea.

MAKING MONEY WITH SERVICES

Services are providing an intangible benefit to the end consumer and are a little more hands-on to execute than products. With services, you are essentially selling hours for money. With the U.S. transitioning from a manufacturing economy to a service-based economy, more and more businesses are moving toward the service-based model, which can be quite lucrative if done properly. If you choose to offer a service, consider these ideas:

Freelance Writing

Everybody needs good content, and the best part is you can write in your spare time. Freelance writers are typically paid by the post or project, so wages vary.

Find a niche by identifying topic areas that you are knowledgeable and passionate about. You will not produce quality work if you are not excited about your subject matter, so make a list of your top 10. Narrow down your list to your top three, and then find 10 publications per passion. These can be blogs, websites, or industry publications. All in all, you should have 30 potential publications you can reach out to.

The next step is to create a website, using WordPress or Squarespace, to highlight your work as a writer. Keep it simple using the following website layout:

1. **About:** Focus on your professional accomplishments.
2. **Portfolio (or Blog):** Highlights of your professional writing work.
3. **Hire Me:** Include the topics you are interested in and a contact form where clients can put their name, email, and subject. Include a rate table once you have built up a large enough portfolio. Look up pricing grids based on the type and length on GhostBlogWriters.com or Scripted.com.
4. **Contact:** Include your social media pages, email address, and telephone number, optional.

For your social media presence, have at least a LinkedIn page for professional networking. Signup for one or more of the following freelancing sites:

- Upwork
- Freelancer

- Fiverr
- Contena
- Mediabistro
- ProBlogger
- WritersWeekly
- PayPerContent
- FreelanceWriting

Also, tell your friends that you are writing on the side for potential referrals.

Don't have a portfolio yet? First, start with a blog that can build credibility, and then you can write for other people's blogs. Your writing should be well-researched, well-written, and delivered on time. Do that so that more work comes in from your first clients. Repeat clients mean you spend less time searching for new gigs and more time earning money. Also, if you incorporate search engine optimization (SEO), you can charge higher fees. The key is to create a habit by setting aside time every day to write.

Rideshare

If you have a car and live in a city, chances are services like Uber and Lyft exist. Instead of using the service, why not be a part of it and generate income on the side? The best part of doing this is you decide when you work. You can do it before work, pick people up on the way to work, work evenings and/or weekends. Be aware of "surge pricing" during high-demand periods like New Years and other holidays. If you time your shift correctly, you can make a lot more than during regular hours. At the time of writing, Uber rates were $1.10 per mile, $0.21 per minute, and $0.80 per trip. The pay structure is simple:

Earnings subtotal=

Base Fare + Time + Distance

For every minute you have a passenger in your car, they are charged. On top of that, every mile you travel is also charged, like how taxis work. If driver supply is low and passenger requests are high, then surge pricing occurs to encourage more drivers to hit the road. This is a multiplier,[46] and its value depends on the gap between driver supply and passenger demand. This is how your fare looks after surge pricing:

Passenger fare=

(Earnings Subtotal x Surge Pricing) + Service Fee

It is important to note that Uber keeps 20% of that total. So, you keep 80% plus any tips the passenger gives you. It is always a good idea to provide excellent customer service so that you get a high rating and potentially a larger tip.

Moreover, keep in mind the costs of running your car, like gas, insurance,[47] and maintenance. A rough rule of thumb is expenses eat up another 20% of your passenger fare, which means after Uber's cut and expenses, you are taking home about 60% of your fare plus any tips. On average, Uber drivers make $15 to $20 an hour,[48] so it can be a way to bring in flexible side income.

Both Uber and Lyft are good starter ideas and offer a "Destination Mode," which basically allows you to make money on your way to and from work by telling the app the direction you are headed and only accept the riders that are along your route. The only limitation with this side business is the money you make is limited to the time you are driving.

Here are a few more tips to make the most out of ridesharing:

- Use the referral and bonus system. The amount varies depending on your location but typically ranges from

$250 to $1,000. This is a big incentive to invite your friends to become drivers as well.

- Use the lowest cost and most fuel-efficient car you can afford. Uber has restrictions, such as having a car that is less than 10 years old, so get something newer but with few miles on it. Saving money on gas is essential when working in ridesharing.

- Aim to drive during surge pricing hours to maximize the money you make.

- Choose trips that involve highway driving since most income comes from per-mile charges.

- Turn on destination mode so that you can take rides on your way to a location you are already planning to go to.

- Provide good customer service to increase the odds of getting a tip. Making money from driving itself can be hard.

Rent Out Your Car Using Turo

If you have a car and rarely use it, rent it out using Turo, an online platform similar to Airbnb for cars. You can rent out your car on an hourly or daily basis. According to their site, the average car sits idle 22 hours a day, so make money on it while it is not being used. The company handles all the insurance. The best part is you do not have to be using your time to drive people around.

For example, say you rent out your car for $40 a day, and your daily expenses amount to $15 a day. You are making $25 a day profit. If you only need your car on the weekends, rent out your car during the week. If you rent your car 20 days a month, then you make $500 a month in profit on one car. If you want to take it a step further, research and see how much it would cost to lease a car compared to your daily rental rate. If you can rent it for more than your lease payment and other expenses, it *might* be worth scaling up this side hustle by leasing cars and then renting them out.

Airbnb

This is an easy and cost-effective way to make extra income. I rent out my condo when I am out of town and have used Airbnb myself on numerous occasions when traveling. If you have a spare bedroom, it is even better since you have more flexibility as to when you can rent it out. Look up the rental rates in your area and see what the average rate is. You may have to start with a lower rate to build up a record of positive reviews. Then, increase your rate over time to match the market. Make sure you have nice photos and a great description of your place. If you are more ambitious and do your research, having multiple properties on Airbnb can bring in a lot of money. Be sure to check to see if Airbnb is permitted where you live. Some condo buildings do not allow it.

Additional service ideas:

- **Tutoring.** You can tutor something related to your work or something you are good at. You do not even need to limit yourself to a local presence if you use a service like WyzAnt.com, which is one of the largest operators in the online tutoring world. If you are proficient at playing the piano, teach piano lessons. If you made a good score on your SAT or GMAT, tutor that. I used to tutor for the CFA exams. The possibilities are endless.

- **Teach English.** You can earn between $14 and $22 an hour teaching English to young students in China with VIPkid.com. The only requirements are that you are eligible to work in the U.S. or Canada, have a bachelor's degree, and a year of teaching experience. Tutoring, mentoring, and coaching all qualify as teaching experience.

- **Delivery Service.** With companies like Uber Eats and SkipTheDishes, you can earn a side income similar to Uber. The average delivery driver makes around $14 an hour. The wage is dependent on how many deliveries are made per hour, which is influenced by traffic, restaurant wait times, and parking.

- **Teaching Online.** If you are knowledgeable about a certain topic, create your own course using Udemy.com or Thinkific.com, and set your own tuition rate. If you already have an online audience, it would be better to sell to your audience directly and save what you would pay to Udemy.

- **Become an Adjunct or Part-time Professor.** You may need a graduate degree for this, but you can make good side income by teaching once a week at your local university or college. A friend of mine teaches part-time and makes about $5,000 a semester per course.

- **Being a TaskRabbit.** TaskRabbit.com is an on-demand errand-running and labor service. You have the freedom to work your own hours in your spare time.

- **Selling on eBay/Kijiji/Craigslist.** First, start with finding things you no longer need and sell them for extra cash. From there, look for market opportunities like going to garage sales and flipping rare finds for a profit. I used to pre-order video game systems and high-demand electronics and flip them. I also sold things for family and friends and took a small cut of the sale, essentially being a virtual eBay merchant. All in all, I sold over $100,000 of products on eBay during my undergraduate days.

- **Selling on Amazon.** Like eBay, if you can find products for cheap, whether you import them or find them at liquidation stores, farmers markets, or garage sales, you might be able to resell them on Amazon for a profit. The nice thing about Amazon is their Fulfillment by Amazon

(FBA) program that allows you to use their warehouse space for a fee, and they will process and ship your online orders for you.

- **Selling on Etsy.** Etsy.com is the world's largest online marketplace for hand-crafted goods. I have numerous friends who knit and craft and then sell on Etsy.

- **Consulting /Coaching.** Consulting is a broad field, but demand for practically every area of expertise exists. What area can you offer advice on that people would be willing to pay you for? Or, another way to look at it is what credentials do you have that give you credibility? Look up what the average rate is for that area and start marketing. It may take some time to develop a reputation and a clientele, but it is worth it. With platforms like Clarity.fm, you can get started quickly and charge up to $60 an hour.

- **Cover Letter and Resume Service.** If you have experience in HR, this can be a great way to make a side income. People looking for a job are willing to have a professional look over their resume and cover letter to provide valuable feedback.

- **Dog Walking.** Providing a service for those who work downtown and have to leave their dog at home in the suburbs can be a lucrative job. Post ads in your neighborhood or, if you are in the U.S., use a site like WagWalking.com. If you are in Canada, use GoFetch.ca. Dog walkers charge between $15 and $25 per day per dog for their services.

- **Pet Sitting.** When homeowners travel, many opportunities exist for pet sitters. In Calgary where I live, doggy daycare centers cost around $40 a day.[49] If you like animals, price your services accordingly and offer great customer service. This gig may be a great way to make additional income.

- **Yardwork.** I used to do this after my day job, working for a school teacher who did this for his side hustle. He charged $10 per lawn to mow once a week, built up his clientele, and at his peak, was mowing over 10 lawns each day after work, and more on weekends. Doing the math, he was making over $1,000 per week mowing lawns in addition to his teaching job. Not too bad!

- **Referee a Sport.** Leagues are always in need of referees, and if you have experience in the sport, it can be a good way to earn money.

- **Blogging.** It takes a lot of work and dedication to build an audience. Like freelance writing, focus on a topic you are passionate about, be it a product review site, a niche you are into, or really anything. WordPress.org offers free templates you can use and set up in no time at all. Typically, posts over 1,000 words get better SEO results so focus on length, and not putting out short low-quality posts.

- **Affiliate Marketing.** Refer website visitors to buy products you recommend online and earn a small commission. It works best if you have personally used the product, whether you do a review on it or recommend it.

- **Child Care.** A nicer way of referring to babysitting, child care can bring in a good side income once you build a client base. If you are in the U.S., use a site like SitterCity.com to find people who need your services. In Canada, look at CanadianNanny.ca.

- **Podcasting.** I am an avid podcast listener and highly recommend them. Over the past year, I listened to over 400 hours of podcasts, and I am not alone. It is estimated that in 2017, over 112 million Americans listened to a podcast.[50] That number is up 11% from 2016, and over 40% of Americans aged 12 and up have listened to one. It is big business. Advertising rates are about $25 to $50 per

1,000 listeners. If you build an audience of 10,000 users, you could make between $250 and $500 an episode. Not bad! Tim Ferriss, the founder of the Tim Ferriss Show Podcast, has the #1 business podcast of all-time, passing 100 million downloads. He is on record saying his podcast makes more than all his books combined.

- **E-Book Publishing.** Whether you use Amazon's Kindle platform, Apple's iBook store, or sell directly from your website, selling e-books on a subject you are passionate about can provide a nice side income. You do not have to be a professional writer or have been previously published to start an e-book. You just need an idea and to start writing! Be sure to get feedback from family and friends, have it professionally edited, and hire a designer for an appealing book cover to boost sales. Another idea is to start a blog first to gauge interest in your topic and then create an e-book based on your blog.

- **Online Dating Specialist.** If you have experience in the online dating realm, you would be surprised at how many wealthy people do not want to spend the time to create a profile, text, and arrange dates. You can do this for them.

- **Home Automation Expert.** The internet of things (IoT) is growing every year, and people want their home connected. Do some research, and you could provide this service to them

- **Website Design.** If you have experience using WordPress, Squarespace, or another website design website, you can charge to create websites for other people. The best part is a lot of the templates offered require zero to little coding experience.

- **Fashion Consultant.** If you are good at matching outfits, why not turn it into a side gig? Help others with their shopping, do a home wardrobe overhaul, and give advice on what colors work. In Vancouver, fashion consultants charge around $100 an hour for their services.[51]

- **Virtual Assistant.** Are you organized and great at scheduling things and arranging travel? Today's entrepreneurs need someone to help them with email, updating databases, creating spreadsheets, and booking travel. Look at sites like PeoplePerHour.com, Zirtual.com, or the other freelancing sites mentioned above.

Pricing Services

A common limitation with services is selling hours for money. The money you make is limited to the hours you put in, and only so many hours are in the day, especially if you have a full-time job. Fortunately, there is a better way to price services. It is called value-based pricing. Value-based pricing is charging a fixed fee that represents the value of the impact your service has on your client. The free online e-book *Breaking the Time Barrier* by Mike McDerment and Donald Cowper dives into this concept in detail. They explain that value is based on the impact you have on the client, which is how they value your services. If you are helping a client with their business needs, say creating a website, the value would be how much money your web design would have on their bottom line. If you estimate your service could provide them with an extra $100,000 of profit annually, then charge accordingly, say $10,000 to $20,000. Most people would invest that amount to make $100,000.

You might be wondering what the logic behind those numbers is? A client is not paying for a collection of hours. Rather, they are paying for the accumulation of skills and talents you have acquired over the years doing what you are doing. If you are first starting out, then charging per hour may make sense while you build up your expertise and credibility. But at a certain point, switch to value-based pricing. Again, the key is providing *value*. When discussing pricing with your potential clients, focus on the value you can bring to them. Thinking about it another way, an hourly rate is not in the best interest of the client because the freelancer's incentive is to bill more hours. It is more beneficial to both parties if value-based pricing is used. You want to sell your value to your client. Since[52] most sites provide online reviews of your work, focus on creating an outstanding customer experience to build a loyal client base and attract new clients.

HOW TO RANK AND SELECT YOUR IDEA

Forecast Your Profit

Estimate your profit for each of your three ideas that you came up with earlier in this chapter. Research what similar existing services charge to get an idea of what you can charge. You are not trying to create a yearly budget with intricate details only a rough sense of *if* the idea is worth pursuing. Your profit is your estimated revenue minus your estimated expenses.

Profit=

Estimated revenue – estimated expenses

Use Projections

Create a range of projections using different revenue assumptions. I normally use a scale—pessimistic, realistic, optimistic— to see what I could potentially make. To keep expectations low, I usually base my goals on the pessimistic scenario. If the idea is still worth pursuing based on the pessimistic scenario, then it may have potential.

How to Rank and Select Your Idea

You learned about feasibility, profitability, and appealability for your ideas. We now add two more factors—scalability and motivation. Scalability is how much time you need to put in to earn a certain income, and motivation is how excited you are about the idea. Putting it in a table like this makes it easier to rank your ideas based on the different criteria:

Your Idea	High	Medium	Low
Feasibility			
Profitability			
Appealability			
Scalability			
Motivation			

As an example, if you own a car and want to use Uber to make additional income but do not like the idea of working evenings and weekends, this is what it looks like:

Idea #1: Uber Driver	High	Medium	Low
Feasibility	X		
Profitability			X
Appealability		X	
Scalability			X
Motivation			X

The feasibility of the idea is high. You have a car and want to use it to make a side income. Appealability is medium since you did your research and noticed that there are not a lot of Uber drivers in your area. Profitability and scalability are low because you are only making money while you are working. Your motivation is low because you do not want to work evenings and weekends when rates are highest.

Idea #2: Turo	High	Medium	Low
Feasibility	X		
Profitability		X	
Appealability		X	
Scalability		X	
Motivation		X	

Compare the Uber idea to using Turo. Keeping everything else the same, it looks like pursuing Turo could be more worthwhile than being an Uber driver. You are paid without needing to physically be in your car, which increased the profitability and motivation factors from low to medium.

What if you decided to write a manual on your Uber driving and Turo experience?

Idea #3: Uber and Turo Online Guide	High	Medium	Low
Feasibility	X		
Profitability	X		
Appealability	X		
Scalability	X		
Motivation		X	

Now, if you decided to write a guide on your experiences with Uber and Turo and sold it online, your initial work would be up-front. Your profitability, appealability, and scalability factors are all high. Appealability increased to high from medium because you are selling guides to anyone who wants them. Motivation remains at medium since writing takes a lot of time and research along with editing to make it useful, but the payoff in the end makes it worth it.

Note that assessing this table matrix is dependent on which of the factors you place the most value on. If motivation and profitability are more important than the other three factors, then place more value on them. The idea that wins is not necessarily the one that has the most "high" ratings, if those categories do not match your priorities. A variation of this table is ranking your ideas from 1 to 10 using the same criteria. Although the more granular you get, the more subjective each rating becomes. I like to keep it high-level when distinguishing the good ideas from the bad.

VALIDATE YOUR TOP 3 IDEAS

Validating your top three ideas is a very important step to avoid wasting your time and money on an idea that nobody wants. Sometimes, we become convinced that we have a great idea before testing the market. Validation is absolutely essential for *saving time and money*. Once you have a list of your top three ideas: Validate, validate, validate.

Share Your Idea

You might be afraid of others "stealing" your idea if you share it. But trust me, this is one of the best ways to see if the idea has legs. Whether the feedback is positive or negative, take it with a grain of salt. After all, you are the one doing the research and hopefully have a better idea if it will sell. Be conscious of ways you can improve your idea. Ideally, test your idea on complete strangers instead of family and friends, who might say they like your idea to be supportive. Do not be afraid of your idea being stolen. 99.9% of the time your idea will not be stolen since it will take a lot of work to implement. And, the execution of the idea is what matters in any event. The feedback will prove invaluable, so share your idea with as many people as you can.

Find Ideas Like It That Already Exist[53]

Most people think that if the idea already exists, then it is too late. In fact, if the idea already exists, it validates that there is a market out there for your idea! Keep in mind what you can do to make your idea a little different or better than the competition to stand out. Having competition is not a bad thing.

Here are a few ideas on how to find ideas that already exist:

- Review top sellers on Amazon. Does it look like there are customers for your product?

- Think of all the things you do daily. Are there any products or services that you use that other people would also?

- Be conscious of the products you use and frequently complain about. Are there any that come to mind?

- Check completed listings on eBay. This gives you a sense of what is selling in the market versus looking at live auctions that may or may not sell. Is there anything that interests you?

- Look for frequent requests on Craigslist. Is there anything that catches your eye?

- Explore popular backed projects on Kickstarter. This is exactly the kind of validation you want to see. Can you create something similar or better?

- See what people want on Reddit. Like reading requests on Craigslist, this gives you an idea of what common issues people have and are willing to pay for. Is there anything you would not mind doing?

Find One Million Potential Customers

Now that you have an idea what people are willing to spend money on, it is time to assess whether you have enough prospective buyers. Use Google Trends, Google Keyword Planner, SEMrush, and Facebook to determine the potential size of your market. See how popular the relevant topic is. If your product is an online course like "Public Speaking 101," then search those terms to see how many hits are showing. If the subject shows over one million hits, then this helps validate your idea.

Drive Traffic to a Basic Sales Page

Tim Ferriss promotes this technique in his book *The 4-Hour Workweek*. It is relatively painless, costs very little, and provides essential feedback to how interested prospective customers are in your idea. First, set up a sales page using Unbounce, WordPress, or Squarespace. Create a few ads to run on Google and/or Facebook, then analyze your conversion rate for ad-clicks and email list sign ups. The prospective customer is not actually buying your product yet. They are simply signing up to your email list to be informed when your product launches. This is how Mint.com launched.[54]

Facebook ads are a similar concept. For $100, you can get about 100,000 people viewing your ad to determine the level of interest based on how many people sign up to your email list.

Sell Before You Build

Driving traffic to your sales page and collecting data is great, but if you are like me, you do not buy everything you say you might. Having a list of 1,000 people who are interested in your product or service is meaningless if none of them pay for it when it launches.

Get around this by creating an optional method to pre-order your product on your landing page for a "champion" or a "VIP" price. If your idea is fully thought out and the only step left is to create it, then the landing page can be a full-on sales page. The more details, the better. These details give your audience more confidence that they will not be ripped off. Be honest that you are still working on the product, but they will be the first to get it once it ships. You can also incentivize a pre-order with part of the product or include a side bonus for people that purchase now.

One last technique is to email 10 people you know to see if they are willing to send you payment. If a few of them buy your product, then you know it is something people are willing to pay for.

SIDE HUSTLE CHECKLIST

Chris Guillebeau recommends using the following checklist before you start selling your idea:

1. **Set up a bank account that is for your side hustle.** The lower the fees, the better. It is important to keep your personal account separate from your side hustle for tax purposes.

2. **Get a separate debit or credit card for your side hustle.** This will also help you keep track for tax purposes.

3. **Pay for everything you can up front.** If your start-up costs are higher than you can afford, think smaller to start.

4. **Set aside at least 25% of your side hustle income for taxes**. The last thing you want is to be dinged at the end of the year and find that the money is already spent.

5. **Be fast with invoicing.** The longer you wait, the longer it will take to get paid.

6. **Insist on a written agreement for service work.** This makes your operation more legitimate and protects you in case of any disagreements.

7. **Think about your legal structure**. For most people, operating a sole entrepreneurship is perfectly fine, but you may want to consider incorporating at a future date.

8. **Set up a simple accounting system.** If you have an accounting system in place from the beginning, it will be less work to keep track of things.

9. **Create a side hustle routine.** Set aside a particular day and time of the week to work on your side hustle to make it easier to be consistent.

10. **Once you are getting paid, set up a day of the month or year to transfer your hard-earned cash into your personal account.** This is the most rewarding part— seeing hard-earned cash transferred into your personal account.

SUMMARY

If you make more money, then you can save more. Start a side hustle for extra income to reach your financial goals faster.

- Look for ideas that are feasible, profitable, appealable, scalable, and motivating to filter the best ideas from the rest.

- The easier the idea is to get started, the better, especially if you can use your current skills or resources.

- Always rank your ideas to select the best ones.

- Validate, validate, validate.

- When pricing products, aim for an 8x to 10x markup.

- For pricing services, start out hourly but convert to value-based pricing once you have enough experience and/or a sufficient track record.

- Use the side hustle checklist before you start your side hustle. Keeping your finances separate and having the appropriate legal structure setup will save you time and headaches in the future.

PART THREE
INVESTING

The first part of this section talks about what stocks are, how to invest in them, what to invest in, what retirement accounts are, and how you can use them to your advantage. I teach you the magic of compound interest, the rule of 72, and dollar-cost averaging, and provide advice on financial advisors and alternative investments.

Later, I break out the American and Canadian retirement accounts, so please read the section that pertains to you. If you live in a different country, apply similar advice to your specific country's retirement accounts. Lastly, I go on to talk about the perils and benefits of real estate, whether owning or renting is better, and other mortgage considerations.

This section is critical for learning how to use the savings you created from the tips in this book to investing in the stock market, where your money will grow indefinitely.

CHAPTER TEN

INVEST IN THE INDEX

STOCKS

first became interested in finance and the stock market when I was 18 working summers with my uncle. He would tell me what stocks were, how to invest, and how much I could make over the years. Excited to make money and thinking the stock market was a gold mine waiting to be plundered, I rushed to the bank, opened a brokerage account, and started investing, not knowing entirely what I was doing. I remember one afternoon my uncle and I were talking about a company that made resin for pipelines. After reading more about the business and their potential for growth, I thought heck what is a few thousand dollars and bought the stock. Years later, the company went bankrupt. Fortunately, I sold at a small loss a few months after purchasing with no idea how much that loss would affect my saving potential later.

"I'm afraid of losing money," some of my friends say. I get that. I have lost money in the stock market, and it hurts. My biggest success came years later when being an Apple fanatic I bought the stock in 2005 and rode it up until 2016 but not without trading it a few times and losing money on a few of them. I ultimately made a lot of money, but those losses ate into my retirement fund. I learned the hard way—do not trade stocks.

Warren Buffett's golden rule of investing is, "Don't lose money." Why is that so important? This chapter talks about the Eighth Wonder of the World: Compound interest and how it is the key to retiring early. Losing money is not cool, but making money is. If your stocks drop 50%, then your money needs to go up by 100% to get back to break even. How can you avoid losing money while investing in the stock market? This chapter explains what stocks are, what you should invest in, and how you will most certainly make money over a long time period.

<u>What Is a Stock?</u>

Think of owning a stock, or a share, as owning a piece of a business. When you own a share, you have the right, but not obligation, to attend the shareholder's meeting for that company, vote on important decisions, and have the right to a share of any future earnings that company makes (hence "share"). This share can be referred to as having equity and entitles you to receive future cash flows of the business, assuming it pays dividends, which is a distribution of a portion of a company's earnings.

Younger companies or companies in their growth phase typically reinvest their profits to help the company grow faster. Start-ups or fast-growing companies do not offer dividends to the public because they are using the profits to grow their business. In theory, this means that in the future they will either pay out dividends or buy back shares, which reduces the number of shares outstanding, increasing the value per share.

When people talk about the "market," they are referring to indexes that track the market, usually the Dow Jones Industrial Average Index or the S&P 500 Index. The Dow Jones tracks 30 of some of the largest U.S. companies, and the S&P 500 includes 500 of the biggest companies traded in the U.S., although not necessarily the 500 largest.

<u>Why Are Stocks So Volatile?</u>

To pay dividends or buy back shares, a company first needs to make a profit and have positive cash flow. Thus, the worth of the dividend or share buyback is ultimately dependent on the profits the company makes over time. No one knows how much money the company will make in the future. Every quarter, analysts try to estimate what profit the company will report and are often wrong. People trying to profit from short-term trades are buying and selling the stock, which can send the stock either soaring or crashing down on a daily basis.

If Stocks Are So Volatile, Why Should I Buy Them?

Depending on your perspective, a company exists to make money for its shareholders or its stakeholders, i.e., employees, community, and shareholders. Successful businesses make more money today than they did yesterday, increasing the value of the stock. Over time, all that speculation and volatility will even out, and the company will likely either pay a dividend, increase a dividend they already pay, use their profits to further grow their business either organically or through acquisitions, or buy back their stock.

Historically speaking, the stock market generally goes up, and dividends increase. The total return varies each year, but over the past hundred years, the stock market has averaged about 10% a year before inflation, with 6% to 8% of that coming in the form of stock price increases and the other 2% from dividend payments. You can receive these payments in cash or have them reinvested to buy more stock, which I recommend.

What About Leaving Money in My Savings Account?

Because of inflation, you lose money every day your money is sitting in your savings account. A savings account typically has a 0.05% interest rate unless you own a high interest rate savings account, which pays around 1.5% (as of 2019, this is subject to change). The average inflation rate in the U.S. and Canada over the past 20 years has hovered around 2% a year, which historically has been low. In 1990, inflation was as high as 6% in the U.S. (Canada 4.8%), and in 1980, it was 12.5% (Canada 10.1%)!

For example, if you kept $1,000 in your savings account with 2% inflation, it would be worth about $980 of purchasing power after one year. Your account would still have $1,000, but the cost of goods you buy, like groceries, would have increased in price by 2% making your money worth less. Multiply that loss each year, and it adds up to a lot of money. How can you beat inflation? The answer is by investing in the stock market.

What Stocks Should I Buy Then?

The right question is not what stock you should buy but how can you buy *all* of them? Warren Buffett, the greatest investor of all time, recommends buying an S&P 500 index fund and doing it consistently. He is on record saying:

"A low-cost fund is the most sensible equity investment for the great majority of investors. My mentor, Ben Graham, took this position many years ago, and everything I have seen since convinces me of its truth."

"Over the years, I've often been asked for investment advice, and in the process of answering I've learned a good deal about human behavior. My regular recommendation has been a low-cost S&P 500 index fund."

"Consistently buy an S&P 500 low-cost index fund. I think that's the thing that makes the most sense practically all of the time."

As wealthy as Warren Buffett is, why not hire an investment advisor to manage his investments instead? The answer is that their fees are too high. Individual stocks cost more to manage, which means advisors take a larger chunk of your earnings. Your financial advisor may charge 2%, which may not seem like a lot, or does it?

Let's say you have $100,000 to invest. Are you willing to pay $2,000 a year plus any additional fees on top of that to your financial advisor? Over 20 years, that is $40,000, not to mention the lost income you could have made if you did not have to pay those fees.

You Have Heard the Stock Market Is Too Risky

You may have heard the stock market is too risky from either a friend or family member. The biggest risk is *not* investing in the stock market. You need your money to outpace the rate of inflation or else you are *losing* money every year. Think about what has happened since 1900:

- First World War
- Great Depression
- Spanish Flu that killed over 100 million people
- Second World War
- Multiple recessions
- Korean War
- Vietnam War
- Cold War
- Gulf Wars
- 1990 Tech Bubble
- 9/11 Terrorist Attacks
- Asian Tsunami
- Great Recession of 2008-2009

If you invested $500 in an S&P 500 index fund in 1901, held on during each major event until 2018, assuming you are still alive, you would have received $7,028,399 back!

Keep Your Emotions Out of It

The average investor makes bad investment decisions. When the stock market is rising, most people feel they need to buy. And then, when markets start falling, they sell. Making money investing is not accomplished by buying high and selling low. It is done by buying low and selling high. Why do we succumb to this instinct when we know better?

Psychologists say that it is because our fear of losing money is greater than our hope for gain. So, when the market has a decline, we panic and sell, which is the worst thing you can do for your returns. I know what you are thinking, "I'm smarter than that! I'm not the average person." I am not either, but guess what, it has happened to me before, and I guarantee that it will happen to you at some point in time unless you listen to this advice.

One of the biggest fund managers, Blackrock, conducted a study on how most investors behaved between 1997 and 2016. The average return for the stock market during this period was 7.68% per year. The average return for the average investor during the same period? 2.29% per year.

That is an underperformance of 5.39% *per year*. If $10,000 was invested, that is the equivalent of receiving $15,728 back on an investment versus $43,924 that the market returned over that same 20-year period.

How did the average investor do compared to other investments?

The average investor not only underperformed the stock market, but they also underperformed **every single investment.** The Dalbar study, one of the longest running and respected research studies in the financial world, determined the four worst times average investors sold:

- 1987 Black Monday Stock Market Crash
- 1997 Asian Financial Crisis
- 2000 Tech Bubble Crash
- 2008-2009 Financial Crisis

In other words, the worst crashes in recent memory.

Investor underperformance is one of the most important reasons to buy the index instead of individual stocks. It would not matter if the stock market is up or down if you are systematically investing. On the other hand, if you buy individual stocks, chances are you will be tempted to buy and sell at the wrong times and devastate your investment portfolio.

INVESTING 101

If you can take away three things about investing other than to invest in the index, remember compound interest, the rule of 72, and dollar-cost averaging.

Compound Interest and The Rule of 72

Albert Einstein called compound interest the Eighth Wonder of the World. What is compound interest? It is the result of reinvesting interest rather than spending it so that interest in the next period is then earned on the principal plus previously accumulated interest, meaning earning interest on interest.

In finance, the rule of 72 is a simplified way to determine how long an investment will take to double given a fixed annual rate of interest that compounds, or multiplies, over time. By dividing 72 by the annual rate of return, investors get a rough estimate of how many years it will take for the initial investment to double. For example, let's say you buy an index that averages 10% growth per year. Expect your money to double every 7.2 years (7 years to keep the numbers easy). If you invest $2,000 when you are 18 years old and retire when you are 60, your money would double six times to become $109,527.

Years	Balance	Amount Invested	Interest Earned
0	$ 2,000	$ 2,000	$ -
7	$ 3,897	$ -	$ 1,897
14	$ 7,595	$ -	$ 5,595
21	$ 14,801	$ -	$ 12,801
28	$ 28,842	$ -	$ 26,842
35	$ 56,205	$ -	$ 54,205
42	$ 109,527	$ -	$ 107,527

You just turned $2,000 into $109,527 by buying the index? YES. It took 42 years, but you only had to invest once and forget about it. That is the magic of compound interest! You can easily turn an investment into multiples of itself over time. That is how people retire at younger ages. ***Invest early and often!***

Dollar-Cost Averaging

Dollar-cost averaging is investing money continuously over your working years, ideally from every paycheck or at least once a month. This is a systematic approach to investing and eliminates the urge to try and time the market. If you try to time the market by either keeping money on the sidelines or selling at the wrong time, meaning missing the best 10 trading days between 1995 and 2014, your annualized returns would drop from 9.85% per year to 6.1%. Better to invest systematically and take your emotions out of the game.

Applying the dollar-cost averaging concept and assuming you invest $2,000 *each year* instead of investing only that first year, your investment would grow to $1,292,329 over the same 42-year time frame.

Years	Balance	Amount Invested	Interest Earned
0	$ 2,000	$ 2,000	$ -
7	$ 24,769	$ 14,000	$ 10,769
14	$ 69,140	$ 28,000	$ 41,140
21	$ 155,606	$ 42,000	$ 113,606
28	$ 324,104	$ 56,000	$ 268,104
35	$ 652,458	$ 70,000	$ 582,458
42	$ 1,292,329	$ 84,000	$ 1,208,329

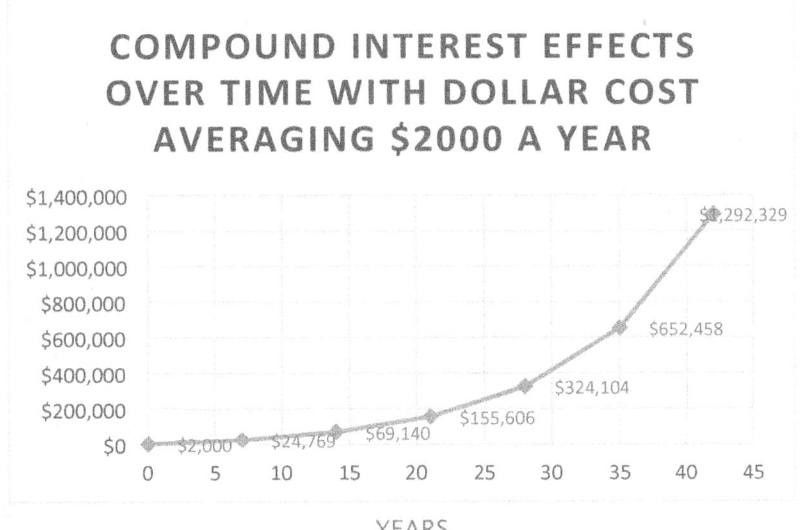

Your investments are worth almost $1,300,000 over the same 42 years, but you only invested $84,000? YUP! That is the power of compound interest combined with dollar-cost averaging. Now, imagine the effects if you save over 30% of your income each year. This is how you can retire early.

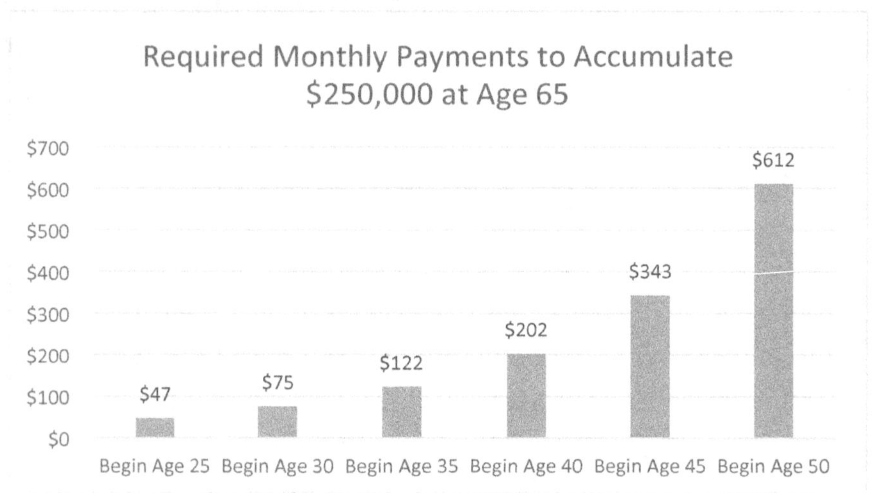

*Assuming 9.7% S&P 500 returns using a compound interest calculator.

In another example, suppose you save $1,000 a year from the age of 25 to 65 in an investment account earning 9.7% a year, which is the average annualized S&P 500 return for the past 50 years, for a total of $40,000. By the time you turn 65, you will have close to $447,572. If you started when you were 35, this would only be worth $170,507. A difference of $277,065.

	Sarah	Sharon
When beginning to invest, the person is...	25	35
Each person invests $1,000 a year for...	40 years	30 years
With a 9.7% rate of return, at age 65, their accounts are worth...	$447,572	$170,507

<u>The Most Important Retirement Chart You Will Ever See</u>

- This retirement chart will inspire you to start saving as much as you can for retirement as soon as you can.

- It can help you decide how much you want to save each year to hit your retirement goal. Remember, you only need to save 25x your annual spending rate.

- It can help you determine how on-track or off-track you are for your retirement goals.

- It can help you set financial goals and make sound financial decisions.

Growing at 9.7% for	$5,000 invested annually	$10,000 invested annually	$20,000 invested annually
5 years	$33,287	$66,574	$133,148
10 years	$86,169	$172,338	$344,676
15 years	$170,181	$340,362	$680,725
20 years	$303,648	$607,297	$1,214,594
25 years	$515,684	$1,031,367	$2,062,734
30 years	$852,537	$1,705,074	$3,410,148
35 years	$1,387,685	$2,775,371	$5,550,741
40 years	$2,237,858	$4,475,716	$8,951,433

For example, let's say your spending rate is $25,000 per year. According to the chart above, if you invested $20,000 per year, you could retire in about 15 years (25 years x $25,000 spending rate= $625,000) using simple index-based investing. Of course, market returns of 9.7% are not guaranteed for the future. However, the concept of compound interest remains the same. Save early and often in index funds, and you will be able to retire a lot sooner than you think.

INDEX FUNDS

Mutual funds and exchange-traded funds (ETFs) are two investment vehicles that allow you to buy a basket of stocks that track the stock index. They have one important difference, however: **Fees**. Mutual funds charge big fat fees, called expense ratios, that eat into your returns, costing investors the equivalent of tens of thousands of dollars over the lifetime of an investment. The justification for the fees is that mutual funds pay managers to pick investments trying to outperform the market. Moreover, some mutual funds charge fees on top of their expense ratio, whether a front-end load (paying a fee when you buy a mutual fund) or a back-end load (paying a fee when you sell a mutual fund). As a result, over 75% of mutual funds do not match the financial returns of the index they are tracking.

ETFs, on the other hand, simply match the market return, keeping their costs low by being passively managed, meaning no managers actively pick the stocks. They are extremely low-cost, easy-to-maintain, and tax-efficient.

In the U.S., a few ETFs seek to replicate the performance of the S&P 500 Index, giving investors several different options. Each has similar returns, so go with the one with the lowest fee structure if your investment account allows for it. I include a few ETFs that cover the Canadian stock market as well, although I recommend buying the U.S. ETFs since the S&P 500 has outperformed the TSX (the Canadian stock market) over time.

Top U.S. Index Funds

SPDR S&P 500 ETF (SPY)[55]

The SPDR S&P 500 ETF (SPY) is the oldest U.S.-listed ETF, having begun trading in 1993 as an innovation in the financial world. Since then, SPY has become one of the largest and widely traded securities in the world with a 9.41% average return for the 10 years between 2008 and 2018 versus 9.52% for the S&P 500.

iShares S&P 500 ETF (IVV)[56]

If you want S&P 500 exposure with a low fee, the IVV is the fund for you. It is plenty liquid, meaning it can be bought or sold with a low transaction fee, with over 1.5 billion shares changing hands every day. Over the past 10 years between 2008 and 2018, it has returned on average 9.44%.

Vanguard S&P 500 ETF (VOO)[57]

The most recent addition to the S&P 500 ETF space came in 2010 with the release of Vanguard's S&P 500 ETF (VOO). While it is only a fraction of the size of the other two ETFs, it has the lowest expense ratio charging just 0.04% per year. VOO only discloses its holdings monthly, not daily like the IVV, which is a slight ding in terms of transparency. And VOO, unlike SPY, reinvests its interim cash. Since its inception, it has a 15.30% average return per year.

"Great," you are probably thinking to yourself, "You just complicated my life with having to choose between three ETF index funds."

I personally recommend investing in the Vanguard S&P 500 ETF (VOO) because it has the lowest fees. You will see later in this chapter how much small fractions of a fee add up over time. I included the other funds just in case some readers want alternatives, or VOO is not available on your platform, although it should be.

Top Canadian Index Funds

FTSE Canada All Cap Index ETF (VCN)[58]

In Canada, the FTSE Canada All Cap Index ETF (VCN) tracks the Canadian market. With an expense ratio of 0.05%, it is cheaper than most mutual funds. Since its inception in 2013, it has a 7.31% average return per year.

iShares S&P/TSX 60 Index Fund (XIU)[59]

iShares S&P/TSX 60 Index Fund (XIU) has exposure to the large, established Canadian companies, is the largest and most liquid ETF in Canada, and started trading in 1990, making it the first ETF in the world. Since inception in 1990, it has returned on average 6.88% per year. The expense ratio is high at 0.18%, however.

iShares CDN Composite Index Fund (XIC)[60]

With iShares CDN Composite Index Fund (XIC), you get to own the entire Canadian stock market and not just the top 60 companies like with XIU. And, it is low-cost with a 0.06% expense ratio versus 0.18% with XIU. Since its founding in 2001, it has returned on average 6.23% per year.

Of the three Canadian market ETFs, I recommend VCN because it tracks the entire market and has the lowest expense ratio. However, if you have a choice, and you certainly do, I recommend the U.S. S&P 500 ETFs over the Canadian market ETFs as over time the U.S. market, which is a more diversified market and home to some of the largest companies in the world, has traditionally outperformed the Canadian market, which is more natural resource-driven. Keep in mind that Americans and Canadians can own any ETF. An American can buy VCN, and a Canadian can buy VOO.

While it is possible to invest in more than one ETF, I do not recommend it because you can be overly diversified with multiple index funds. The upside is that you may add a layer of safety, but that may come with sacrificing returns. I recommend buying the lowest-cost U.S. index fund for the greatest return.

Watch Out for Fees

The average mutual fund fee, called an annual expense ratio, is 0.89%. While this may not sound like a lot, it will erode gains in your investment portfolio compounded over time.

For example, if you invest in a mutual fund that earns a 7% annual return but has a 2% expense ratio, your investment would only grow by 5%.

In comparison, the average fee for an index fund is 0.12%. Say you want to invest $1,000 per year in a market index growing at the market average of 9.7% a year for 30 years. Should you choose an account with a 0.89% or 0.12% fee? While the fee differential looks small, it adds up.

Management Fee	Amount in Your Account 30 Years from Now
0.12% fee	$166,514
0.89% fee	$143,159

Of the $23,355 difference, $9,958 was due to fees, but the biggest impact was the compounding effect on your return. Over $14,000 was lost in compounding potential! Since your money is growing at a slower rate because of the fees, your money will grow slower and slower compared to a fund with lower fees. And this example looks at two relatively low-fee funds. Some funds have an expense ratio that is over 1%, which will eat into your returns quickly. When deciding which index fund to invest in, look at the fees.

ADVICE ON FINANCIAL ADVISORS

The common conception is that because financial advisors and stock-picking fund managers invest for a living that they are better at it than the average person. This assumption could not be further from the truth.

According to a 2016 research report from Standard & Poor's, over the past 15 years, 92.2% of large-cap funds lagged a simple S&P 500 index fund. The percentages of mid-cap and small-cap funds lagging their benchmarks were even higher: 95.4% and

93.2%, respectively. In other words, you have a 1 in 20 chance, or 5%, of beating the market when investing outside of an index, and this includes financial advisors.

In 2005, Warren Buffett made a wager of $500,000 that no professional could select a portfolio of at least five hedge funds, meaning funds that actively manage money, that would match the S&P 500 index over a 10-year period. Only one investment manager decided to take him up on the challenge. The results were not even close. The five hedge funds as a group managed only a 2.2% annualized return, compared with a 7.1% average return for the S&P 500 index fund. Buffett estimated that 60% of fund gains went to the management fees *even though they dramatically underperformed the market.*

A study in 1973 by Paul Slovic, a world-class psychologist and peer of Nobel prize winner Daniel Kahneman, demonstrated that the more information we have, the worse decisions we make. This is counter-intuitive to the common belief that the "better informed" we are, the better our decisions. Accumulating information is believed to give an advantage in most fields if not all. In his study, he found the opposite can be true.

Slovic gathered eight professional horse handicappers and asked them to predict the winners of horse races. These handicappers made their living using their gambling skills and as such were highly experienced. Slovic told them they needed to make predictions on 40 horse races in four consecutive rounds. For the first round, each gambler received five pieces of information on whatever they wanted to place their bet. This could be anything from how old the horse was, to years of experience of the jockey, and so on.

As another facet to the study, Slovic also had the handicappers say how confident they were in their predictions. There was an average of 10 horses per race, so each handicapper should be correct about 10 percent of the time, and so their confidence with a blind guess should also be 10 percent.

So, what happened? After the first round, with only the five pieces of information, the handicappers were 17 percent accurate, which is pretty good. They were more accurate than a blind guess. What is more fascinating is that their confidence was 19 percent, which almost matched their accuracy of 17 percent.

The second round introduced more information. For the second round, the handicappers were given up to ten pieces of information on anything they wanted to help them determine the winning horse. The third round they were given 20 pieces of information and in the fourth round 40 pieces of information. Logically, we would assume the more information they had, the more accurate they would be. However, their accuracy stalled at 17 percent. Having 40 pieces of information did not improve the odds of their winning over having five pieces.

What about the confidence in their predictions? Their confidence nearly doubled to 34 percent. The more information they had did not improve their accuracy, yet the handicappers felt they had an advantage that boosted their confidence.

Why is this the case? We typically make a decision and then try to justify it with information that confirms our original assessment. We tend to ignore or dismiss any information that conflicts with our conviction. Psychologists call this "confirmation bias," and it is evidenced in multiple fields and studies.

Relating this back to investing, an almost limitless amount of information exists. Trying to keep on top of it all is a recipe for disaster. Who is to say that the reasons for the dollar continuing to go lower is a direct consequence of monetary policy or trade relations with China and so on? You hear it all the time that the financial experts cannot explain why stocks continue to go higher or lower. It is hard to make sense of so many moving pieces, and the harder we try, the more we can succumb to confirmation biases. It is better to ignore the noise and expert opinions on the stock market and invest on your own with your money in a stock market index.

More Information = Analysis Paralysis

Not only does having more information give us a false sense of confidence in the world of investing, but we are likely to become paralyzed by the information and make no choice, which is just as bad or worse than making the wrong choice. Barry Schwartz writes in his book *The Paradox of Choice: Why More is Less*:

"...As the number of mutual funds in a 401(k) plan offered to employees goes up, the likelihood that they will choose a fund – any fund – goes down. For every 10 funds added to the array of options, the rate of participation drops 2 percent. And for those who do invest, added fund options increase the chances that employees will invest in ultraconservative money-market funds."

How often have you stood at the supermarket wondering which toothpaste to buy? Investing can be the same thing—overwhelming. There are so many choices that many people simply do not invest, or if they do, they make a hasty decision ending in lower returns. The same factor affects financial advisors and their stock picking ability.

Financial Advisors Are Human

Financial advisors are prone to the same behavior biases as regular people. Just like with anyone, the more confident someone is, the more they are prone to overconfidence, leading to disastrous results.

Do you need a financial advisor? If you follow my advice, then no you do not. But depending on your level of comfort with your finances, you may want a financial coach. A financial coach is a fee-only professional who charges you a flat fee. The fee-only system removes any potential conflict of interest. Someone on commission is incentivized to make you buy and sell to make money, which is how most financial advisors are compensated.

<u>No One Can Predict the Future</u>

The next time you hear an analyst talking on TV about what she or he thinks the stock market is going to do, change the channel. No one knows what the stock market is going to do.

> *"Forecasts may tell you a great deal about the forecaster; they tell you nothing about the future."*
>
> —Warren Buffett

The best thing you can do is to invest early, often, in stock indexes, and use dollar-cost averaging over time whether the market is moving up or down. **Most likely, you will make more money over the long term.** Otherwise, if you listen to analysts and financial advisors, chances are your portfolio is going to under-perform.

HOW DO I BUY?

You can open a brokerage account with your bank or use an online brokerage. Before you open an account, consider these factors:

- **Commissions:** Almost all online brokers charge a trade commission, normally between $5 to $10 per trade.
- **Account fees:** These include annual fees and inactivity fees.
- **How often you plan to buy:** If you are buying the index ETF monthly, as you should, you want a broker with low commissions.

- **Support:** Brokers offer various levels of educational re-sources and customer support.
- **Minimums:** A broker's minimum can range between $0 and $2,500 or more.

Once you decide on a broker, signing up for an account will require:

- Social Security ID (U.S.) or Social Insurance Number (Canada)
- Driver's license or other government-issued ID
- Address
- Employment status
- Annual income and net worth
- Date of birth. Note: Most require you to be over 18.

You need to send a deposit or funds transfer, which is often the minimum amount. The funds' transfer can take between a few days and a week. Once the funds are transferred, you can begin investing. To invest, search for the ticker symbol for the index fund you want to buy, say VOO, which is the Vanguard S&P 500 ETF and has the lowest expense ratio, and decide how many shares to purchase. Once you hit buy, you are finished. Do this once a month or every paycheck for the rest of your working life, and you will have nothing to worry about in your retirement.

Personally, living in Canada, I like dealing with RBC with their online trading platform. I can easily transfer funds between accounts, often instantly, and I can set up automatic withdrawals to other accounts to make it easier to save. They also offer an account where you can practice buying and selling stocks. A lot of the other Canadian banks offer the same services.

If you are in the U.S., it might be worth checking if your bank offers the same services. Otherwise, open an account at E-Trade, TD Ameritrade, Merrill Edge, or Robinhood to name a few. You can also open an account with a robo-advisor, which I go into later in the chapter.

ALTERNATIVE INVESTMENTS

But what about your friend who made a 50% gain on cannabis stocks or the friend of a friend who keeps talking about cryptocurrencies and tripled his money? These are the two biggest investment topics when writing this book, but replace them with whatever is being talked about now. The fact is that it is very hard to beat the market year after year. Your friend may beat the market this year, next year, and the year after that, but because all his or her eggs are in one basket, it just takes one problem with the industry or company, and they could underperform the market or even lose it all. Just like flipping a coin, someone can flip heads five times in a row but then have the sixth flip come up tails.

Gold

Gold is another popular investment for those people fearing the end of fiat currency or for those seeking a *safe* investment. A quote from Warren Buffett on gold:

"Gold gets dug out of the ground in Africa, or someplace. Then we melt it down, dig another hole, bury it again and pay people to stand around guarding it. It has no utility. Anyone watching from Mars would be scratching their head."

Gold has no utility. It is used in very limited quantities in the world for jewelry, coins, dental fillings, and decorative items, and that is about it. Should you buy gold? Wharton Finance Professor Jeremy Siegel keeps track of various asset class' returns from 1802. Siegel calculated that if you bought $1 worth of gold in 1802, it would be worth $3.11 today. In comparison, if you bought $1 of the stock market index in 1802, it would be worth $1,033,487. I would not recommend buying gold and neither would Warren Buffett.

Alternative investments, in general, tend to be subject to trends, fads, manias, and erratic investing behavior, so be careful.

Real Estate

Real estate is not a very good investment for most investors. Why? Because returns are poor, and over time the average return on property has been 0% after taking into account inflation. The exception to this is that if you receive more rental income than your payments and have positive cash flow, then it can be a good investment. I discuss real estate at length in Chapter 12: The Perils & Benefits of Real Estate.

Penny Stocks

Penny stocks are typically shares of a company that trade for under $1 per share, hence the name. Often people are drawn to penny stocks because they fluctuate in value in very short periods of time. You could see a penny stock rise from $0.10 to $1.00 overnight, with many thinking, "Wow, if only I put in $10,000, it could be worth $100,000." Little do they know that penny stocks are akin to gambling. Most companies trading for those prices have little to no earnings, most investors lose money, and the stocks are purely speculative with many susceptible to pump and dump scams, and furthermore, they often have poor management teams. The stock of the company is trading at low prices for a reason, and if something sounds too good to be true, it often is. It is better to wait and see if the company can prove itself before investing, or better yet, buy the index and avoid penny stocks altogether.

WHAT ABOUT ROBO-ADVISORS?

A robo-advisor is a service that uses highly specialized software to do the job of wealth managers or investment advisors—people who decide what investments you should be making and then tinker with those investments over time. You typically fill out a questionnaire to determine your appetite for risk and then, through proprietary algorithms, spread your money into various investments, adjusting over time as your situation and the market changes. They primarily invest in ETFs and typically collect under 1% in annual fees, which is less than a professional investment advisor who can charge as high as 3%.

Should You Invest with a Robo-Advisor?

They are completely safe, and there are ways to ask questions through their customer service support. Overall, however, I recommend you open your own investment account(s) at your bank, set up automatic withdrawals, and invest in a single ETF that tracks the entire S&P 500 index as mentioned earlier. The reason why I recommend you invest on your own is again the *fees*. While robo-advisors charge less than mutual funds, on average, they still do what you could do for less.

For example, Betterment's lowest fee option is 0.38% per year versus the Vanguard S&P 500 ETF 0.05% fee. Moreover, the lack of control you have and the variety of ETFs offered can hinder your returns. Why invest in an alternative investment ETF when you can invest in the S&P 500 index with a proven track record over time of nearly 10% a year in returns? Furthermore, many robo-advisors do not offer financial advice other than investing and will not help you with tax planning, budgeting, or other financial planning.

Lastly, some robo-advisors might not consider your outside accounts. For example, if you have a 401(k) or RRSP where your employer matches, this is the best place to invest first. Many robo-advisors, however, do not include those assets in their planning, which can skew and unbalance your portfolio.

I only recommend investing with a robo-advisor if you do not want to deal with the small hassle of investing in an index fund yourself or will otherwise be checking your investment account every day and be tempted to day trade the market, which is one of the best ways to destroy your returns. Compared to human financial advisors, robo-advisors can be a good deal with *advisory fees* between 0.25% and 0.50%, which is less than half of what human financial advisors charge, and an *investment fee* of 0.08% to 0.13%, for a total of 0.33% to 0.63% of your portfolio per year.

If you choose to go the robo-advisor route, do your research. I recommend Wealthfront simply because it offers the lowest fees. For Canadians, Wealthsimple ranks near the top of the list and typically in the top three. Use the online calculator at autoinvest. ca to see which robo-advisor is recommended based on what you consider important criteria.

WHAT ABOUT BONDS?

A bond is an IOU either issued by a company, government, or some other institution. When you buy a bond, you essentially lend money to the organization, your "principal," in return for an interest payment that you receive either monthly or quarterly. The term of the bond varies from one day to over 30 years. The interest you receive is called a "coupon."[61] At the end of the term, you receive your principal back. Bonds are generally minimal risk because you only lose your money if the company or government goes bankrupt. If you buy a government bond, they can always print more money, so this is often referred to as the risk-free rate of return.

Generally, rich people and old people like bonds because they are such a safe, low-risk investment, and typically, your funds are locked away for the term of the bond. You may have heard that you should subtract your age from 100 and that is the percentage of your investment money that should be in stocks, and the rest should be in bonds. I do not necessarily agree with this advice, but it depends on your risk tolerance and how many years away you are from retirement. In almost all circumstances, the stock market has outperformed bonds over time. Bonds, on average over the past 80 years, have given a 5.2% return on average versus close to 10% for stocks. If you are in your 20s or 30s, I highly recommend having a 100% stock index portfolio. If you are older, I still recommend a stock index portfolio, but depending on your risk tolerance, you may want to consider mixing your portfolio with bonds.

If you are having a hard time deciding on your asset allocation, remember the 4% withdrawal rate and the Trinity Study in Chapter 3: Save 25X Your Annual Spending Rate. It showed that if you have an investment portfolio consisting of 50% stocks and 50% bonds, then you could withdraw 4% of your investment portfolio each year in retirement without fear of running out of money. If you have a 100% stock portfolio, you could withdraw 5% of your portfolio without drawing down your savings over 70% of the time, and a 6% withdrawal rate without drawing on your savings 55% of the time. If you have $1 million saved up in retirement and a 50/50 portfolio split, you could withdraw $40,000 per year safely. With a 100% stock portfolio, you could withdraw up to $60,000 per year.

SUMMARY

Avoid keeping money in savings accounts. Inflation will eat away the value of the cash. Instead, invest in ETFs that match the stock market return to keep your money from becoming devalued over time and allow you to grow your retirement nest egg.

- Remember the power of **compound interest**, the **rule of 72**, and **dollar-cost averaging**. These concepts allow you to retire early when applied properly.

- Avoid financial advisors because they are human just like you and are susceptible to confirmation biases like everyone else.

- Complexity is the enemy of execution, so keep it simple. Invest in one index fund ETF.

- Keep your emotions out of investing and invest for the long term. Directly trading stocks will harm your returns.

- Watch out for the fees when investing in ETFs. Every 0.01% difference will save you thousands of dollars over the years.

- Avoid alternative investments that are fads and/or high risk and real estate.

- If you are rich or older, bonds can be good to incorporate into your investment portfolio. Otherwise, if you are young and have time on your side, a 100% stock portfolio will provide greater returns with compound interest.

- If you choose to use a robo-advisor, do your research and remember you are paying for the convenience.

CHAPTER ELEVEN

USE YOUR RETIREMENT ACCOUNTS

WHY RETIREMENT ACCOUNTS ARE IMPORTANT

Picture this. You are on the first day of your new job, fresh out of undergrad, filling out forms when you come across the 401(k) section. You think to yourself, "I can always start saving later. Besides, I have a lot of bills and could use the money." Ten years later, you start a family and think, "I'll start saving when I have fewer bills or when I get the next raise or promotion." Flash forward to age 40. Your kids are grown, you are making a lot of money, and have few bills to pay. FINALLY, you can save.

If you start saving now, by some estimates, you need to save more than a third of your salary just to *catch up*. When you were 22, the Dow Jones Industrial Index was at 1,800. As I write this, it is at 23,000. You could have made over 15x your money over that time. The right thing to do, then, is to sign up to your 401(k) or equivalent on the very first day you start your new job! And consider, some companies match 401(k) contributions, so you lost out on free money.

These accounts, called retirement accounts, are used to save and invest money for retirement. They offer benefits that include acting as a tax shelter to minimize taxes owed on investments and tax-deferred growth, meaning investments continue to grow tax-free and compound over time. Every country is different, but the concept remains the same, using specifically designed accounts to help you with your retirement savings. They are important because government-sponsored plans can no longer be relied upon as a sufficient sole source of retirement income.

In the U.S., Social Security is no longer enough to retire on. In the 1980s, Social Security could make up about half of people's pre-retirement income. For someone retiring now, it covers only about 40%, and over time, that percentage will continue falling.

The Canadian Pension Plan (CPP) is not much better. If you retire at the age of 65 in Canada, expect to receive between $641 and $1,134 a month, or $7,692 and $13,608[62] per year from the Canadian Pension Plan. It is better to apply for CPP later and receive more, depending on if you have the savings in the meantime. If you wait until you are 70, you receive 42% more per year than if you start taking CPP at 65. The average life expectancy is increasing every year. On average, Americans who reach the age of 65 can now expect to reach age 84.

There are many different investment accounts: 401(k)s and IRAs in the U.S. and RRSPs and TFSAs in Canada. What if you chose the wrong account or invested in the wrong thing?

This chapter is slightly technical. So, if you do not need to know the specifics, then skip to the section "The Money Allocation Order" for Americans and Canadians.

The data in the chapter is based on the rules for 2018. Keep in mind that limits on retirement accounts change every year. So, search the web for the latest information.

In the case of personal bankruptcy, most of the money in retirement accounts is off limits from creditors. Another perk is retirement accounts are often excluded when college financial aid offices determine how much a family can pay for college.

AMERICAN ACCOUNTS

Whether you work for an employer or own your own business, you have access to some tax-favored plan. If you work for an employer, you will likely have a 401(k) plan or 403(b) if you work for a non-profit. For simplicity's sake, I refer only to 401(k)s from this point on because a 403(b) is essentially the same. If you work on your own, you can open an individual retirement savings account (IRA). The differences between them are:

- 401(k)s are retirement accounts available to most employees of a company or non-profit.

- IRAs are available to the self-employed and those who work for an employer that does not offer a 401(k).

Each account has benefits that I will discuss in more detail. The idea with these accounts is that your money is left alone over the years so that it can compound over time.

With a 401(k), your employer typically narrows down the investment options for you whether it is an actively managed fund, index fund, bond mutual fund, international fund, or money market fund. Watch out for the fees, however. Often, company 401(k) plans invest in terrible, high-fee funds, so look at where your money is going.

IRAs are a little more involved since it is up to you to choose the type of investment that it will go into. The best option is almost always a stock index fund.

With either account, your funds are locked away until you are 59½. If you withdraw early, you will be hit by Uncle Sam and subject to a penalty.

401(K)S

One of the most important things to know about 401(k)s is that most employers match your investment up to a certain percentage. For example, you can put in 3% of your salary, and your company matches it. That is the same thing as saying you are getting a **100% return on your investment!** Nowhere else will you receive the same return, so it is *imperative* that you start contributing to your 401(k) if you have not already. And remember the concept of compound interest? You want to invest as much as you can the earlier you can.

Here are some scary facts about employees age 25 and under in the U.S.:

- Less than a third participate in a 401(k),
- Less than 4% max out their contributions, and
- Only 16% contribute enough to get the full company match.

There are some reasons for this. For private sector employees aged 22 and younger, 41% have no access to a 401(k) through their employer, compared to 35% of Gen Xers and 30% of baby boomers.[63] This is not an excuse not to save. If your employer does not offer a 401(k), open an IRA.

Also note that while a 401(k) is one of the best ways to save for retirement, it has restrictions. Typically, when a company matches your contributions to the plan, you cannot tap into those immediately. There is a vesting period, which is the amount of time you must work for your company before gaining access to its payments to your 401(k). Think of it as an incentive to stay at your job for a few years. Your contributions always vest immediately. So even if you leave your job before your employer contributions vest, you keep your money.

The IRS mandates the contribution limits for 401(k) accounts. Look up the current contribution limit for your tax year before contributing.

Two different 401(k)s exist: Traditional 401(k), which is more common, and Roth 401(k). Chances are your company offers a Traditional 401(k). Read about each below to determine which one you should invest in.

Traditional 401(k)

Most large employers have the option of saving money in a Traditional 401(k). These accounts essentially offer two tax breaks— one up front and the other over the long term. First, you do not have to pay taxes on the money you contribute to a 401(k). This is known as a **pre-tax contribution**.

For example, if you earn $60,000 a year and contribute $5,000 to a Traditional 401(k), you are only taxed on $55,000 that year. If you are in the 20% tax bracket, you save $1,000 that year in taxes.

The second tax break is not needing to pay taxes on the interest your investments make over time, which is a substantial amount over 40 years. You are only taxed when you withdraw at retirement, saving you thousands of dollars.

Roth 401(k)

The Roth 401(k) is relatively new, so not all employers offer it. However, it has grown in popularity since its first release in 2006. With a Roth 401(k), you make an **after-tax contribution**, meaning you pay with after-tax dollars. So, you pay taxes on your money as you normally would, and then after you make your contribution, you never pay taxes on it again, even when you start making withdrawals. In other words, you cannot deduct your contribution from your income and pay less tax up front. Rather, you save on taxes when you withdraw at retirement.

How Your 401(k) Grows

Let's say you are 25 and start investing $5,000 a year, and your employer matches $5,000 per year into an index fund growing at 10% per year.

Age	Your Contribution	Employer Match	Balance Without Employer Match	Balance with Employer Match
25	$5,000	$5,000	$5,500	$11,000
30	$5,000	$5,000	$41,631	$75,209
35	$5,000	$5,000	$100,625	$188,280
40	$5,000	$5,000	$195,635	$370,384
45	$5,000	$5,000	$348,650	$663,662
50	$5,000	$5,000	$595,082	$1,135,991
55	$5,000	$5,000	$991,964	$1,896,681
60	$5,000	$5,000	$1,631,146	$3,121,780
65	$5,000	$5,000	$2,660,555	**$5,094,814**

By age 40, your investment with employer matching would grow to $370,384 compared to $195,635 without the match. And by the time you turn 65, you would have a little over $5 million compared to $2.6 million if your employer did not match, a difference of over $2.4 million! And, this assumes you are not paying into an IRA on top of that.

Should I Invest in a Traditional or Roth 401(k)?

If you think that you will pay a higher tax rate in retirement, then opt for a Roth 401(k) so that you can pay taxes now at a lower rate. Otherwise, choose a Traditional 401(k).

If you start with a Traditional 401(k) and want to switch to a Roth 401(k), some employers allow this but not vice versa. This transition is known as a Roth 401(k) conversion.

Tip: When you change jobs or retire, you can roll your 401(k) into a Traditional IRA. You might want to do this because of the wider investment selections available with IRAs, like index funds or funds with lower fees. IRAs also are more flexible for withdrawals relating to a first-time home purchase or education expenses. But be careful because if the company cuts a check payable to you, 20% of the funds will be withheld for taxes. If you were planning to make a tax-free rollover, you must fund the amount taken by the IRS and put it into an IRA within 60 days or else any portion of the payout not rolled into an IRA within that time will be considered a taxable distribution.

The best route is a direct rollover from the 401(k) custodian, or trustee, to the IRA. A custodian or trustee is often an employee of the company, but companies can hire outside service providers to handle the recordkeeping and administration of the plan. That way, the money never reaches your hands, and there is no risk of triggering an accidental tax bill. You can only make one IRA rollover a year. Furthermore, be careful with the fees associated with rollover IRAs because they are often higher than workplace retirement plans and can eat into your savings.

Tip: If your company goes out of business, do not worry. Your 401(k) is off limits. The plan will most likely be terminated, in which case you can roll your 401(k) over into a Traditional IRA to avoid paying the 10% withdrawal penalty and income taxes. Withdrawing from a 401(k)

You do not have to start withdrawing from your 401(k) until you turn 70½. Withdrawals are technically referred to as "distributions" and should only be used as a last resort. However financial emergencies happen, so keep this in mind:

- If you withdraw from a Traditional 401(k) early, defined as before the age of 59½, then all the money is subject to income taxes and a 10% penalty.

- If you withdraw from a Roth 401(k) early, you can withdraw your contributions tax-free, but your *earnings* are subject to income taxes and a 10% penalty. You must be over 59½ and have had your account open at least five years,[64] which is counted from the day you make your first contribution, to withdraw without incurring income tax and the 10% penalty on earnings withdrawals.

Borrowing from a 401(k)

With a 401(k) loan, you can withdraw up to $50,000, or half the vested balance in your account if it is less than that. You then repay your account over a period of up to five years. You will pay some interest on the amount withdrawn, and most 401(k) plan providers and platforms charge fees to process and service the loan. This adds to the cost of borrowing and repayment.

Another thing to consider is that your employer may not offer these loans. Your odds are better if you work for a larger company, many of which now include 401(k) loans as part of their retirement package.

While borrowing from your 401(k) might be an option, it should only be considered in a true financial emergency, otherwise you sacrifice years of compound interest and retirement savings, drastically extending how long you need to continue working before retiring.

Switching Employers

If you are tempted to cash out a 401(k) when switching employers, consider these four reasons for why[65] you should not:

1. It Is Unnecessary

If you switch employers, you do not have to make any moves with your 401(k). You can keep the money in your old company's plan and let it continue growing at that tax-deferred rate. There are, however, drawbacks, like no longer being able to contribute to it and the admin fees. But if the plan is better than the one your current employer offers, leaving your money behind can be the best move.

2. Fees and Taxes

The early withdrawal penalty also applies to cashing out your 401(k). If you ask your retirement provider to liquidate your account and send you the proceeds, you pay that fee to the IRS if you are under the age of 59½. You also pay income taxes on it, which can add another 10% to 37%.[66]

3. Rolling Over Is Easy

Rolling over your retirement plan from your previous employer to your new employer or an IRA is an effortless process. Your new HR department will have a form that you fill out to allow them to pull the funds and reinvest them. You avoid both income taxes and the dreaded 10% early withdrawal penalty.

4. Lost Growth Potential

Each $10,000 withdrawn and spent could be worth $64,870 in 20 years.[67] It is better to roll over your investment to your new employer or an IRA, and let it grow tax-free.

	Traditional 401(k)	Roth 401(k)
Contributions are	Pre-tax	Post-tax
Can be started by	Employer only	Employer only
Maximum annual individual contribution	$18,500 (2018)	$18,500 (2018)
Can roll-over to	New employer's Traditional 401(k), Traditional IRA, or Roth IRA	New employer's Roth 401(k) or Roth IRA

Pay taxes at	Withdrawal at retirement	Time of contribution
Can begin withdrawing earnings without penalty	At age 59½	At age 59½
Taxes in account	No taxes on dividends, capital gains, or interest.	No taxes on dividends, capital gains, or interest.

IRAS

IRAs are another form of retirement account, although employers do not offer them. IRAs are private accounts set up through mutual fund companies, banks, and brokers. Even if you have a 401(k), you can still open an IRA.

The maximum the government allows you to contribute to an IRA, as of 2018, is $5,500 per year plus an additional $5,500 to your spouse's IRA if he or she does not earn any income. If he or she does work, they can contribute $5,500 to their own account. These limits apply to your total IRA contribution, whether you contribute to a Traditional or Roth IRA.

Traditional IRAs

This is like a Traditional 401(k) except you are responsible for the account. As with a Traditional 401(k), you deduct your contribution from your income, meaning an "up-front" tax break. The Traditional IRA's up-front tax breaks are called **deductible IRAs**. You only pay taxes with the withdrawals at retirement, which allows your money to grow tax-free and compound over the years. This process is called "tax-deferred growth."

For example, if you earn $60,000 a year and contribute $5,000 to a Traditional IRA, you only pay taxes on an income of

$55,000. If you are in the 20% tax bracket, you save $1,000 in taxes that year.

If your employer does not offer a 401(k), then in almost all circumstances, you can contribute up to the full $5,500 limit to your Traditional IRA. The one exception is that if you are married to someone who has an employer 401(k) plan. In this scenario, you can only make the full contribution to a Traditional IRA if your combined annual income is $186,000 or less (as of 2018), and you and your spouse file a joint return.

What if your employer already offers a 401(k)? You can instead make the full $5,500 annual contribution to a Traditional IRA if:

- You are single, and your adjusted gross income is $62,000 or less, or

- You are married, file jointly, and your adjusted gross income is $99,000 or less.

If you are married and file separate tax returns, you cannot claim the full deduction no matter what your income is.

Roth IRAs

Just like with Roth 401(k)s, you do not have the up-front tax break on your contributions. Also, as with the Roth 401(k), it will grow tax-free for life. Even when you withdraw in retirement, you will not pay taxes.

Like with Traditional IRAs, you can open a Roth IRA even if you already have a 401(k) at work. As of 2018, you can make the full $5,500 annual contribution to a Roth IRA if:

- You are single, and your adjusted gross income is $118,000 or less, or

- You are married, file jointly, and your adjusted gross income is $186,000 or less.

You can still have a Roth IRA even if you have a higher income, but the amount you can contribute will be less than the full $5,500.

You can still make a partial contribution if:

- You earn under $133,000 as a single person, or
- You earn under $196,000 as a couple filing jointly.

It varies depending on income. Research online to see what your partial contribution can be.

Ask yourself these questions when trying to determine whether to invest in a Traditional or Roth IRA:

Do You See Yourself in a Lower or Higher Tax Bracket in Retirement?

The reason to invest with a Traditional IRA before a Roth is that you will likely be making less money in retirement and thus be in a lower tax bracket than you would be with your after-tax contribution with a Roth IRA. If you think you will be making more money in retirement and be at a higher tax bracket, then invest in a Roth IRA instead.

What if You Need to Withdraw Funds in the Next Few Years?

With Roth IRAs, you can withdraw your contributions at any time without penalty. The earnings, however, are a different story. However, this is inadvisable since you should keep your money in as long as possible to grow tax-free. If you feel you may be tempted to withdraw in a non-emergency, keep your money in a Traditional IRA. Since withdrawals face a 10% penalty, the cost will serve as motivation to keep the funds in place. If you feel you might need the money for an emergency, then a Roth IRA provides greater flexibility.

What Is Your Financial Situation?

The choice between a Traditional or Roth IRA often comes down to your financial situation. If you are financially stretched, consider taking an immediate deduction with the Traditional IRA. You can use the savings to pay down other debts or pursue another financial goal. If you feel more financially confident, choose the Roth IRA. But whatever you do, make sure the deposits are automatic so that you spare yourself the hassle at tax time.

Withdrawing from an IRA

First, you do not have to start withdrawing from your IRA until you turn 70½. Withdrawing from an IRA depends on what kind of IRA you have.

- For Traditional IRAs, you pay income tax and a 10% penalty on withdrawals before the age of 59½.

- For Roth IRAs, you can withdraw your *contributions* at any time without paying any taxes or paying the 10% penalty fee. Your *earnings* from your Roth IRA are taxed when you make an early withdrawal before the age of 59½ and before you have held the account for at least five years. Earnings are defined as any withdrawals that exceed your total contributions. Also, your account must be open for at least five years,[68] starting from the day you made your first contribution, to avoid incurring tax and the 10% penalty on earnings withdrawals.

There are exceptions to paying taxes on Roth IRA withdrawals on your earnings, called qualified distributions, but you need to have the account open at least five years without incurring the early withdrawal 10% penalty and taxes. If you have your account open for at least five years, then you can avoid taxes and the penalty on your earnings for the following reasons:

- Higher education costs for you, your spouse, or your children.[69]

- Unreimbursed medical bills, if they exceed 10% of your adjusted gross income, or health insurance premiums you pay while you are unemployed.

- Home buying costs, which can include a down payment or closings costs, of up to $10,000. This is the lifetime cap per person, reserved for people who have not owned a home in the past two years.

- You become disabled.

If a withdrawal is not a qualified distribution, then you will also have to pay income taxes on top of the 10% early withdrawal penalty.

You can also borrow money from either a Traditional or Roth IRA and put it back within 60 days without paying taxes or the 10% penalty, but this should be used as a last resort. If you fail to pay back the full amount, you will pay taxes and the penalty on the **entire** amount of the withdrawal. So, borrower beware!

Tip 1: Many tax deadlines fall at the end of the year, but IRAs are an exception. You can make prior year IRA contributions up until April 15 of each year.

Tip 2: If you move money from one IRA to another, e.g., to switch company's or consolidate accounts, request a direct transfer from one custodian, or trustee, to the other. There is no limit on direct transfers.

	Traditional IRA	Roth IRA
2018 contribution limits	**$5,500; $6,500 if age 50 or over**	**$5,500; $6,500 if age 50 or over**
Contributions are	Pre-tax	Post-tax
Pay taxes at	Withdrawal at retirement	Time of contribution
Withdrawal rule	Withdrawals before the age of 59½ are subject to income tax and a 10% penalty. Withdrawals are penalty-free beginning at age 59½. Withdrawals must begin at age 70½. Beneficiaries pay taxes on inherited IRAs.	Contributions can be withdrawn at any time, tax-free and penalty-free. Five years after your first contribution and age 59½, earnings withdrawals are also tax-free. No withdrawals are required during the account holder's life time. Beneficiaries can stretch distributions over many years.
Taxes in account	No taxes on dividends, capital gains, or interest.	No taxes on dividends, capital gains, or interest.
Extra benefits	In some cases, up to $10,000 penalty-free withdrawals to cover homebuyer expenses, but taxes are due. Qualified education and hardship withdrawals are also available.	After five years and in some cases, up to $10,000 of earnings can be withdrawn penalty-free to cover homebuyer expenses. Qualified education and hardship withdrawals may be available without penalty before the age 59½ and the five-year waiting period. These may be taxed.

CANADIAN ACCOUNTS

In Canada, the two primary investing accounts used for retirement is the RRSP and TFSA. Both can be opened with your investment brokerage and shelter your investments from taxation, allowing your money to grow tax-free using a variety of investment options. In some ways, they are the opposites of each other, but each should be used simultaneously to meet your retirement goals.

- The RRSP, the older of the two, was introduced in 1957. Best to use if you feel your taxation rate will be lower in retirement than it is now to maximize your savings. It is more restrictive regarding withdrawals as you cannot take out money penalty free unless you are buying your first home or education purposes. Some employers offer pension-matching contributions for RRSP contributions, which is a nice benefit.

- The TFSA was introduced in 2009. Best to invest in if you feel your taxation rate will be higher in retirement than it is now to maximize your savings. It is also more flexible, allowing you to withdraw funds at any time, which can be a benefit or hindrance to your long-term retirement savings.

It is ideal to take advantage of both accounts to maintain flexibility and maximize your savings. I go further into detail below.

RRSPS

RRSPs, or Registered Retirement Savings Plans, are a tax-deferred investment vehicle. You do not pay tax on the contributions but do pay tax when the money is withdrawn, typically in retirement. You pay taxes on the withdrawn money as income rather than the more favorable capital gains and dividend tax rates. However, the fact that the money grows tax-free should offset any downside from paying taxes on withdrawals in retirement. You can also invest in many types of investments within an RRSP: cash, stocks, bonds, money market funds, mutual funds, and index funds.

Annual Contributions[70]

Contribution limits exist with RRSPs. To find out the exact amount you can contribute to your RRSP for the current year, check your most recent Notice of Assessment you received from the Canada Revenue Agency. You may contribute to your RRSP until December 31 of the year in which you turn 71. The following limits and deadlines apply:

Historical RRSP Maximums:

- 2013: $23,820
- 2014: $24,270
- 2015: $24,930
- 2016: $25,370
- 2017: $26,010
- 2018: $26,230

Your allowable RRSP contribution for the current year is the lowest of:

- 18% of your earned income from the previous year,
- The maximum annual contribution limit for the taxation year, or
- The remaining limit after any company-sponsored pension plan contributions.

Earned income includes salary or wages, alimony received, and rental income, among other income sources, but does not include investment income.

Company Pension Plan or Deferred Profit Sharing Plan

If you have a company-sponsored pension plan or are part of a deferred profit sharing plan, the amount you can contribute to your RRSP must be reduced by the total value of the pension credits you earned for the year. This amount is referred to as a pension adjustment (PA), and you will find it on the Statement of Remuneration Paid (T4 slip) that you receive from your employer.

Annual Contribution Deadline

To qualify for an RRSP deduction for your current taxation year, you can make contributions any time during the year or up to 60 days into the following year.

Carry-Forwards

If you cannot contribute to your maximum-allowed annual contribution, you can carry the difference forward. The amount of your unused contribution limit is shown on your federal Notice of Assessment. You may also decide to delay claiming your current year's RRSP tax deduction. To choose to take the deduction in a later year, make sure that your allowable deduction limit has not been reached.

Over Contributing to Your Plan[71]

Any contributions over your RRSP contribution limit for the year is considered an over contribution with a lifetime allowance of $2,000 without being penalized. However, you cannot claim a deduction for the excess amount, meaning you cannot claim it for a tax refund.

If you over contribute by more than $2,000, you are subject to a 1% penalty tax for each month you are in excess, up to 12% a year. Be careful to not over contribute!

Withdrawing from an RRSP

First, you do not need to start taking money out of your RRSP until the year you turn 72, although many people start withdrawing when they retire.[72] Even so, by December 31 of the year you turn 71, you need to decide whether to cash out your RRSP (or wait until you turn 72), purchase an annuity from an insurance company (not recommended), or transfer your RRSP to a registered retirement income fund (RRIF). For young people, RRSP withdrawals typically happen in one of three situations—purchasing a home, withdrawing for education, or financial difficulty. I would highly recommend not withdrawing from your RRSP even if you are facing financial difficulty because you are borrowing from your future and seriously harming your retirement nest egg. That leaves two other reasons for withdrawing early without paying taxes.

Two Reasons to "Borrow" from Your RRSP Tax-Free

1. You can withdraw $35,000 tax-free for a down payment through the **first-time home buyer's plan (HBP)** if you have not owned a house in the past four years. You then pay this back to your RRSP over a maximum of 15 years. If you do not follow the repayment plan, then the withdrawals are added back to your income, and you must pay taxes on the money. Note that you must have the funds in your RRSP account for a minimum of 90 days before you can withdraw them under the HBP.

2. You can also withdraw up to $10,000 per year, up to a max of $20,000 total, from your RRSP for education expenses under the **Lifelong Learning Plan (LLP).** You would pay this back to your RRSP over a maximum period of 10 years. Like the HBP, if you do not follow the

repayment plan, then the withdrawals are added back to your income, and you will pay tax on them. The amount you withdraw is not limited to the amount of your tuition or other education expenses. If you meet all the LLP conditions when you make the withdrawal, you can use the funds you withdrew for any purpose. While $20,000 is the total overall limit, once this is completely paid back, you can participate in the LLP again.

Before you decide to borrow from your RRSP, weigh the pros and cons. There is no right or wrong answer as it is entirely dependent on your situation. To help with your decision, ask yourself these questions:

- Will you be able to repay the requirement amount back each year?

- Is it the right time to cash out your RRSP? Note, this depends on the investments and rate of return you are getting on your current investment.

- Is it worth forgoing the future tax-sheltered growth potential of your RRSP in favor of reducing the mortgage amount or education expenses?

Outside of withdrawing from your RRSP under the HBP and LLP, if you choose to withdraw from your RRSP early, there are tax consequences.[73]

1. You Pay a Withholding Tax

For any early withdrawals, your financial institution will hold back the tax on the amount you take out and pay it directly to the government on your behalf. The withholding tax varies between 10% and 30% depending on how much you choose to withdraw from your RRSP. In Quebec, these rates are higher.

If you withdraw:	Withholding tax rate outside Quebec	Withholding tax rate in Quebec[74]
Up to $5,000	10%	21%
Between $5,000 and $15,000	20%	26%
More than $15,000	30%	31%

For example, if you withdraw $25,000 from your RRSP early, after the 30% withholding tax ($7,500) is applied, you only end up with $17,500.

2.   The Amount You Take Out Is Taxable Income

You must report the amount you take out on your tax return as income. At that time, you may have to pay more tax on the money, on top of the withholding tax. It depends on your total income and tax situation.

RRSP Pros

- You receive a tax refund that you can reinvest in the market.
- RRSPs force you to save for the long term.
- RRSPs are a good investment vehicle for those with high incomes during their working years, assuming they will be in a lower tax bracket during retirement.
- Some employers offer RRSP matching.

RRSP Cons

- If you make more money in your retirement than during your working years, which can happen more easily than you think between receiving your RRSP, Canada Pension

Plan, and other income, then your tax bracket in retirement will be higher, and you will pay that tax rate on your withdrawals.

- Your money is locked in until you retire, except for using the Lifelong Learning Plan or Home Buyer's Plan.

- If you do not earn much money the year you contribute, you will not get much of a tax refund. It is better to use a tax-free savings account (TFSA).

- If you do not reinvest your tax refund, you lose out versus investing in a TFSA.

TFSAS

Tax-Free Savings Accounts (TFSAs) are an amazing investment vehicle, especially if you are young. You contribute after-tax dollars and never pay tax again on the money, regardless of how much it grows. You have the flexibility of withdrawing the money, and then receiving that *contribution room* back the following year. But be careful! Because of the flexibility of withdrawing funds, people often use this account as a short-term savings account. Treat a TFSA as a retirement account and avoid withdrawals to allow your money to grow tax-free.

Annual Contributions

The contribution room changes every year. Increases are indexed to inflation and rounded to the nearest $500. Your contribution room is made up of:

- Your TFSA dollar limit plus indexation,

- Any unused TFSA contribution room from the previous year, and

- Any withdrawals made from the TFSA during the last year.

Historical TFSA Limits:

Year	TFSA Annual Limit	TFSA Cumulative Limit
2009	$5,000	$5,000
2010	$5,000	$10,000
2011	$5,000	$15,000
2012	$5,000	$20,000
2013	$5,500	$25,500
2014	$5,500	$31,000
2015	$10,000	$41,000
2016	$5,500	$46,500
2017	$5,500	$52,000
2018	$5,500	$57,500

Every year, the cumulative TFSA contribution limit grows for everyone over the age of 18.

Let's assume it is 2018, and you just turned 18. If you open a TFSA account today, your contribution limit will be $5,500. If you turned 18 before 2009, your contribution limit is $57,500.

You can invest in any investments with a TFSA, just like with an RRSP. This means cash, stocks, bonds, mutual funds, money market funds, and index funds.

Carry-Forwards

Your unused contribution room can be carried forward indefinitely, and there is no limit on how much contribution room you can accumulate.

Over Contributing to Your Plan

Just like with an RRSP, a penalty will be assessed by the Canada Revenue Agency of 1% per month if you over contribute, up to 12% a year. Ouch! Unlike an RRSP, there is no $2,000 lifetime over contribution limit.

Withdrawing from a TFSA[75]

Depending on the type of investment held in your TFSA, you can typically withdraw any amount at any time, which makes it way more flexible than an RRSP. All withdrawals are tax-free. Another benefit of tax-free withdrawals is that they have no effect on your eligibility for certain government tax benefits such as Old Age Security (OAS), which can be reduced if you earn higher income levels, including receiving money from your RRSP.

Important to note that when it comes to withdrawing from your TFSA, making a withdrawal does not result in lost contribution room. Any withdrawals you make this year will be added to your unused contribution room next year.

Also, and this is very important, you cannot contribute more than your TFSA contribution room even if you make a withdrawal during the year. The withdrawal does not reset your limit. You must wait until the beginning of the following year when the amount you withdrew is added back to your unused contribution room.

TFSA Withdrawal Example

Date	Action	Available Contribution Room
January 8, 2017	Claire turns 18 and opens a TFSA	$5,500
July 29, 2017	Contributes $3,500	$2,000
August 7, 2017	Withdraws $1,500	$2,000
October 1, 2017	Contributes $1,100	$900
December 3, 2017	Withdraws $500	$900
January 1, 2018	New contribution room available	$8,400

In the example above, Claire starts with $5,500 in contribution room because that was the TFSA contribution limit for the year 2017. Notice that as she made contributions to her TFSA throughout the year, her available contribution room decreased by the same amount. However, when she made a withdrawal, the contribution room stayed the same.

In 2018, her contribution room consists of 3 things: The TFSA contribution limit made available to her, her unused contribution room from the year before, and the withdrawals she made in the prior year. Putting these numbers together, she gained $5,500 in contribution room for 2018, had $900 in unused contributions from 2017, and she withdrew a total of $2,000 from her TFSA in 2017. This gives her $8,400 in contribution room for the year 2018.

2018 contribution room=
$5,500 (2018 limit) + $900 (remaining from 2017) + $2,000 (2017 withdrawals)=
$8,400 contribution room for 2018

TFSA Pros

- It is a flexible investment vehicle that allows you to withdraw your money at any time, tax-free, and without penalty.

- When you retire and start withdrawing money from your RRSP and TFSA accounts as well as collect other benefits like CPP and Old Age Security, the government does consider your TFSA withdrawals when "clawing back" Old Age Security payments.

TFSA Cons

- Tax-free savings accounts are misconstrued as being only "savings accounts." A savings account pays very little interest. You can invest in any number of investments with a TFSA, so use it for this purpose.

- Most people earn more during their working years than during their retirement, which can give an RRSP the edge but only if the tax refund is invested.

- The temptation to withdraw money from your TFSA is real. Making withdrawals will hinder your long-term investment performance.

TFSAS VS. RRSPS

For example, assume you make $1,000 per year before tax. This table shows how a TFSA contribution is made with after-tax dollars, while withdrawals are tax-free. An RRSP contribution is made with pre-tax dollars, while withdrawals are taxable.

	TFSA	RRSP
Pre-tax income	$1,000	$1,000
Tax (assuming 40%)	$400	N/A
Net contribution	**$600**	**$1,000**
Value 20 years later @ 9.7% growth	$3,822	$6,370
Tax upon withdrawal (40%*)	N/A	$2,548
Net withdrawal	**$3,822**	**$3,822**
*The marginal tax rate is the rate of tax charged on the last dollar of income.		

This also shows that if your marginal tax rate at the time of the RRSP contribution is the same as at the time of the withdrawal, TFSAs and RRSPs work out equally well, if and only if the tax refund from the RRSP is reinvested. But there is one problem, typically most people spend the RRSP refund and do not reinvest it as they should. In that case, the TFSA will almost always be the better choice.

If Your Marginal Tax Rate Is Lower in Retirement

	TFSA	RRSP
Pre-tax income	$1,000	$1,000
Tax (assuming 40%)	$400	N/A
Net contribution	**$600**	**$1,000***
Value 20 years later @ 9.7% growth	$3,822	$6,370
Tax upon withdrawal (25%**)	N/A	$1,593
Net withdrawal	**$3,822**	**$4,777**
*Assumes $400 tax refund is reinvested (40% of $1,000). ** Assumes a lower tax rate in retirement.		

In the above example, the marginal tax rate in retirement is 25%, less than the initial 40% during the person's working years. The RRSP comes out ahead when the $400 tax refund is reinvested.

Not Reinvesting the RRSP Refund

	TFSA	RRSP
Pre-tax income	$1,000	$1,000
Tax (assuming 40%)	$400	N/A
Net contribution	**$600**	**$600***
Value 20 years later @ 9.7% growth	$3,822	$3,822
Tax upon withdrawal (25%**)	N/A	$956
Net withdrawal	**$3,822**	**$2,866**
*Assumes $400 tax refund is reinvested (40% of $1,000). ** Assumes a lower tax rate in retirement.		

In the above examples, the RRSP beat out the TFSA when the tax refund was reinvested *and* the tax rate was lower in retirement. The TFSA beat out the RRSP if you did not reinvest the RRSP refund. Using this logic, invest in a TFSA first, and RRSP second if you feel you will not be able to reinvest the refund.

Note that contributing to an RRSP does not guarantee a refund, but contributions will reduce taxes owed, which is essentially the same idea. However, the downside to a TFSA is it is very flexible for withdrawals and may lead to temptations to raid it over the years. In that case, RRSPs are the better choice due to the severe early withdrawal penalties, for anything but withdrawing for a down payment or education purposes. Furthermore, TFSAs typically have lower contribution limits per year than RRSPs.

	TFSA	RRSP
Contribution limits	You start collecting contribution room the year you turn 18, and the annual limits are set by the CRA. The limit for 2018 is $5,500.	Your maximum contribution limit is 18% of your earned income up to a maximum amount set by the CRA. The maximum contribution limit for 2018 is $26,230.
Contributions are	Post-tax	Pre-tax
Withdrawals	You can withdraw funds from your TFSA at any time without paying taxes.	Withdrawals from an RRSP will be treated as taxable income for that year with a few exceptions.
Contribution room	You can recontribute whatever amounts you have withdrawn starting in the following calendar year.	Withdrawals cannot be added back to the contribution room.

Consequences of over-contributing	You will pay a 1% penalty of the over-contributed amount for every month that your TFSA contains excess funds.	You can make a cumulative over-contribution of $2,000 to your RRSP in your lifetime with no tax penalty. After that, you are charged 1% of the over-contribution per month.
Accounts	Can be open as long as you live, and contributions can made indefinitely.	You can only have an RRSP open until you turn 71. After that, you must convert your RRSP into a registered retirement income fund (RRIF), use the funds to buy an annuity, or withdraw all the funds.

THE MONEY ALLOCATION ORDER

The order to allocate your money is similar for both the U.S. and Canada. Typically, you want to establish an emergency fund. Then, max out the contributions your company matches with a 401(k) or company pension. Next, pay off your credit card debt first, followed by tax-free retirement savings accounts, and finally a direct-managed investment account if you have extra cash.

1. Establish an emergency fund.
2. Contribute to your 401(k) or company pension up to their match.
3. Pay off your credit card debt.
4. Max your Traditional or Roth IRA contributions if you are in the U.S. In Canada, max your TFSA contributions.
5. Max your 401(k) contributions in the U.S. In Canada, max your RRSPs.

6.   Invest any remaining cash in a direct investing account.

If you live in the U.S., step 4 can be to max your health savings account (HSA). HSA funds are completely tax-free when used for medical expenses, making the HSA better than either traditional or Roth IRAs for that purpose.

If you expect your marginal tax rate to be higher in retirement, invest in your IRA before maximizing your 401(k) because withdrawals are tax-free. In Canada, max out your TFSA before your RRSP.

If you expect your marginal tax rate to be lower in retirement, invest in your 401(k) and RRSPs first.

Always invest any tax refunds from the government back into an investment account.

Why this order? You need an emergency fund to provide enough flexibility just in case the unexpected happens. The last thing you want to do is to dip into your investments when the market is down. You want to contribute up to your company match because this is the highest return you can get on your money, which can be 50% to 100% depending on their match policy.

Credit cards are next. You immediately receive a 15%+ gain on your investment through savings on interest payments.

Then, you want to invest in your IRAs or TFSAs because your investments will grow tax-free. Also, you will not be tempted to spend the cash refund from the government you would receive with an RRSP or equivalent.

Then, you want to max your 401(k) contributions or RRSPs. Finally, if you have any remaining cash, open a direct investing account and keep saving!

AVOID WITHDRAWING

If you can help it, **never take money from a retirement account**. The only exception is if you are taking out money for a down payment on a house or using it for education. In these cases, look up the limitations and calculate if it is worth the lost investment potential. Many people dip into their retirement savings at one point or another, which can be a fatal mistake for their retirement. Not only will they be paying taxes on it, in the U.S., they will also be charged another 10% withdrawal fee. This penalty is meant to keep your retirement funds where they belong, in your retirement account, so that you can save for retirement.

SUMMARY

Whether you live in the United States or Canada or anywhere else in the world, retirement accounts are essential to help you achieve your retirement goals. With the benefits that governments give, which include tax breaks allowing your money to grow tax-free and compound over time, using these accounts to your advantage is essential.

In the U.S., whether you choose a Traditional 401(k), a Roth 401(k), a Traditional IRA, or a Roth IRA, the concept of saving money remains the same. If you find it hard to choose, open a 401(k) and an IRA to maximize your saving potential

In Canada, open an RRSP and TFSA, and know the pros and cons of each. Below is a quick summary of the various accounts and why you should use them.

I also include the American and Canadian Money Allocation Order at the bottom. If you live outside of North America, adjust accordingly.

UNITED STATES

- If you expect your marginal tax rate to be higher in retirement, then invest in a Roth 401(k). Otherwise, invest in a Traditional 401(k). Some employers allow you to switch from a Traditional 401(k) to a Roth 401(k) but not vice versa.

- It is advisable to have both a 401(k) and IRA account.

- Know the annual contribution limits for each investment account.

- Never withdraw from your retirement accounts if you can help it. You are seriously harming the compound interest potential if you withdraw anything.

- If you face a financial emergency, an alternative to pursuing an early withdrawal from your 401(k) is to borrow from it. You can do this anytime and for any reason and pay back the money within five years without penalty.

- If you have a financial emergency and need to withdraw from your retirement accounts, know the criteria when you can withdraw without paying taxes and/or a penalty:
  - Traditional 401(k): Any early withdrawals before the age of 59½ will be subject to income tax and a 10% early withdrawal penalty.
  - Roth 401(k): You can withdraw your contributions tax-free, but your earnings are subject to income taxes and a 10% penalty.

- If you leave your employer, either keep the funds in the retirement account or have them rolled over into your new employer's investment plan. Avoid cashing out.

- Traditional IRAs: Any early withdrawals before the age of 59½ are subject to income tax and a 10% early withdrawal penalty.

- Roth IRAs: You can withdraw your contributions anytime without penalty. Any earnings withdrawn before the age of 59½ are taxed except for the following qualified distributions if you have had your account open for at least five years:
  - Higher education.
  - Unreimbursed medical bills exceeding 10% of your adjusted gross income or health insurance premiums you pay while you are unemployed.
  - Home-buying costs, which can include a down payment or closings costs, up to $10,000.
  - You become disabled.

CANADA

- Having both an RRSP and TFSA is recommended.

- Generally, if you reinvest the RRSP refund and expect to have a lower tax rate in retirement than you currently pay, the RRSP is preferred. Furthermore, it is less likely that you will withdraw from an RRSP early. So, using this logic, it is advisable to invest in an RRSP before a TFSA. However, if you think you will spend the RRSP refund or you think your tax rate will be higher in retirement, then the TFSA is the better option.

- Always reinvest the RRSP refund.

- If you have a financial emergency and need to withdraw from your retirement accounts, know the criteria when you can withdraw without paying taxes and/or a penalty:

  - RRSPs: You can withdraw without penalty for the following reasons:

    - First time home buyer's plan (HBP): You can withdraw $35,000 tax-free for a down payment if you have not purchased a home in the past four years. You will have to pay it back over a maximum of 15 years.

    - Lifelong Learning Plan (LLP): You can withdraw up to $10,000 per year, to a maximum of $20,000 total, from your RRSP for education purposes and pay it back over a maximum of 10 years.

  - TFSAs: You can withdraw any amount without penalty.

The Money Allocation Order:

1. Establish an emergency fund.

2. Contribute to your 401(k) or company pension up to their maximum match.

3. Pay off your credit card debt.

4. Max out your Traditional or Roth IRA contributions if you are in the U.S. In Canada, max your TFSA contributions.

5. Max out your 401(k) contributions in the U.S. In Canada, max your RRSPs.

6. Invest any remaining cash in a direct investing account.

CHAPTER TWELVE

THE PERILS & BENEFITS OF REAL ESTATE

HOME OWNERSHIP

The United States and Canada have some of the highest levels of homeownership in the world. More interesting is that in many Western European countries homeownership does not have the same appeal. For example, about 50% of German households[76] own a home compared to 65% of Americans[77] and 68% of Canadians.[78] More facts about homeownership:

- New York, Vancouver, Los Angeles, and Toronto have some of the most expensive real estate in the world.

- Canada and the United States have some of the highest levels of debt in the world.

- Interest rates are low (today), which has helped boost real estate prices.

You do not have to be a rocket scientist to figure out that the housing market in these cities could be in a financial bubble. I hear it all the time, especially regarding Vancouver and Toronto. When is the market going to crash? Is it going to crash? It is hard to say, but keep in mind that house prices do not always go up. Recall the 2008-2009 housing market crash. Rising interest rates will not help either.

For most Americans and Canadians, their home is or will be their largest financial asset. It is also a leveraged asset, meaning most people need a mortgage to buy their home. This means when real estate prices rise or drop, it can have a substantial impact on your net worth.

For example, if you own a $250,000 home and have $25,000 of equity in it, all it takes is a 10% drop in the housing market for you to lose all your equity. Also important to note: If you have problems making your mortgage payments, you risk losing the house plus everything you put into it.

RENTING VS. BUYING

Is owning real estate always a good idea? Yes, and no. On the one hand, it is a kind of forced savings. You are making mortgage payments instead of rent payments and are paying down the principal each month. On the other hand, it is an expensive savings plan. Not only is your mortgage payment likely higher than your rent, depending on the city you live in, but you have other hidden costs of homeownership. Think about repair and maintenance expenses than can often cost 1% or more annually. You also pay mostly interest for the first few years of the mortgage and property taxes each year. Do not assume home prices will increase every year, and if so, on average, they do not increase more than inflation. The word mortgage is derived from Old French and roughly translates to "an agreement till death." That does not sound appealing to me, but to others, it may.

The alternative is to rent a place that is cheaper than a mortgage and invest the difference in index funds. You will build more wealth faster this way as you will receive a higher return on the money you would have used as a down payment and be able to retire sooner. The only problem with this approach is most people spend the difference between what they are saving on rent and what they would have paid on a mortgage. Another risk is that rents could rise. Many people spend more than the recommended 25% of income on housing. So, what should you do? Buying a house is a great thing when you are settling down in a place you want to live for the next 10 years, that is convenient, and where you are okay with several hours a month of maintenance work.

Saving Money on Rent

Keep in mind that you want housing to be less than 25%, ideally 10% to 20%, of your take-home pay. So, if you rent and want to save money, try the simple tactic of asking for lower rent. This approach is best done after living at your place for a year, proving you are a good tenant. The landlord may prefer to lower the rent to keep you rather than risk getting a bad tenant for $50 or $100 more a month. Again, this cannot be done in all cities, but it is certainly worth trying. If you have a spare bedroom or basement suite, look to sublet that space. Subletting is the practice of an existing tenant renting out their place or extra room to a subtenant. If you choose to pursue this option, first obtain your landlord's permission, or else your rental agreement could be void. If your landlord agrees, do the appropriate background checks and ensure you have a signed, legally binding sublease contract with the subtenant.

REAL ESTATE CAN BE A POOR INVESTMENT

Real estate, if you are not careful, can be a poor investment. First, if your house is your biggest investment, how diversified is your portfolio? If you pay $1,500 a month in mortgage payments, are you offsetting that by investing $4,500 a month in other investments to balance your risk?

Second, real estate, on average, offers a poor rate of return for investors. Yale economist, Robert Shiller, found that "from 1890 to 1990, the average return on residential real estate was close to zero after inflation."

Third, over the course of a 30-year mortgage, you pay nearly double the selling price because of the interest.

We constantly hear about people making money in real estate. It is not that easy, though. For one, it depends on which city you live in, and by the time you hear someone is making money, it is probably too late to invest.

As an example, say you bought your house for $200,000 in cash, and it doubled to $400,000 over 10 years. You made over $200,000. But let's look at the fees associated with owning it and selling it:

- Realtor at 6% commission: $24,000

- Property taxes over the 10 years: $20,000, assuming $2,000 a year

Total cost= $44,000.[79] You made at most $156,000 over 10 years, or a 5.8% annual return[80] for a total return of 78%.

Another cost most people do not consider when investing in real estate is the opportunity cost of investing in real estate versus the stock market. Let's say you took that $200,000 and put it into an S&P 500 index fund instead. At a 9.7% average annual return, your investment would be worth $504,773, for a total return of 152% or $304,773, meaning you missed out on $148,773.

You may argue that the benefit of real estate is using leverage to your advantage and borrowing with a mortgage versus paying cash. However, this assumes real estate will appreciate over time, which is not guaranteed. Remember, one of the reasons why property values have increased in some cities is because interest rates decreased to record lows after the 2008-2009 housing crisis and debt rose to record levels. This is not likely to continue forever.

The same could be said with the stock market, but if you buy an index fund, you are more diversified than owning a single property and have fewer costs involved in case you need to sell your investment. Moreover, the above example implied real estate prices increased by 7.2% per year when they are more likely to rise at the inflation rate. If inflation is 2% per year, then the house would be worth $243,798 over 10 years with the realtor fees and taxes eating into all the gains if you were to sell.

But wait, what about saving money when you make your mortgage payments? You are paying down your principal as a form of saving, but you can do the same thing by renting a place that costs less than a mortgage payment plus principal pay down. Do not think of your home as an investment—it is a shelter. If your rent payment is equal to a mortgage payment, then owning is better. However, there is an alternative, an easier method to having exposure to real estate without going through the costs of having a mortgage.

INVESTMENT ALTERNATIVE TO OWNING A HOME

If you want real estate investment exposure without buying a property, owning a REIT, which stands for a Real Estate Investment Trust, is a low-cost way to get it without paying realtor fees, transaction fees, and everything else that comes with purchasing a property. Furthermore, they are highly liquid, meaning you can buy and sell freely, and they can be contained in your investment account as part of a diversification strategy.

What is a REIT? REITs are companies that own or finance income-producing real estate in a range of property sectors. Most REITs trade on major stock exchanges and offer several benefits. REITs are required to distribute at least 90% of their taxable income to shareholders as taxable dividends. I suggest putting REITs in a retirement savings account to avoid taxes.

Think of a REIT as a mutual fund focused on real estate. They allow anyone to invest in a portfolio of real estate assets that can include condominiums and commercial real estate, like shopping malls, offices, hotels, and much more. You buy shares in a REIT and are paid dividend distributions.

In general, the same economic factors that increase the stock market impact the performance of REITs. An expanding economy, job growth, and investment in the economy will lead to increased prices for both. A contracting economy, decline in the employment level, and reduced investment will have the opposite effect. Keep in mind that REITs traditionally perform better in low-interest rate environments since most of the properties are leveraged with debt because lower interest rates mean more income distributed out as dividends. If interest rates are increasing, then your returns might not be as high as they have been historically.

What are the returns like for REITs?[81] Between December 31, 1978 and March 31, 2016, total returns for exchange-traded U.S. Equity REITs have averaged 12.87%[82] compared to 11.53% for the S&P 500 over the same period.[83] Not too shabby. But watch out for the volatility. The magnitude[84] of gains and losses with REITs outpaces those of the S&P 500, so they are not for the faint of heart.

Overall, I recommend keeping it simple and buying the S&P 500 index. However, if you want some real estate exposure without purchasing a property, consider these REIT ETFs, which I discuss for the U.S. and Canada separately, although you can purchase any REIT with your investment accounts.

U.S. REITs

Vanguard REIT ETF (VNQ)[85]

VNQ is at the top of the list for broad, diversified exposure and a reasonable expense ratio of 0.12%. Its goal is to track the return of the MSCI U.S. REIT Index, a gauge of real estate stocks. Since its inception in 2004, it has on average returned 6.00% annually after taxes.

Schwab U.S. REIT ETF (SCHH)[86]

SCHH invests in REITs from the Dow Jones U.S. Select REIT Index, and its goal is to track that index as closely as possible, before fees and expenses. Since its inception in 2011, it has on average returned 6.39% annually after taxes.

iShares U.S. Real Estate ETF (IYR)[87]

IYR invests mostly in ETFs and attempts to keep 90% of its assets in securities that are in the Dow Jones U.S. Real Estate Index. The emphasis on the fund is on the large-cap players. Since its inception in 2000, it has on average returned 6.98% annually after taxes.

Canada REITs
iShares S&P/TSX Capped REIT Index Fund ETF (XRE. TO)[88]

XRE aims to generate long-term capital growth by tracking the S&P/TSX Capped REIT Index. XRE provides exposure to 15 different REITs across diversified, retail, residential, and commercial properties. Since its inception in 2002, it has on average returned 9.86% annually.

BMO Equal Weight REITs Index ETF (ZRE.TO)[89]

ZRE aims to generate long-term capital growth by tracking the Solactive Equal Weight Canada REIT. ZRE provides exposure to 18 different REITs across diversified, retail, residential, and commercial properties, with a focus on diversified, residential, and retail. Since its inception in 2010, it has on average returned 10.1% annually.

Vanguard FTSE Canadian Capped REIT Index ETF (VRE.TO)[90]

VRE aims to generate long-term capital growth by tracking the FTSE Canada All Cap Real Estate Capped 25% Index. VRE provides exposure to 19 different REITs across diversified, retail, residential, and commercial properties, with a focus on industrial, office, retail, and residential. Since its inception in 2012, it has on average returned 6.96% annually.

Should You Buy a REIT ETF?

REITs are:[91]

- Easy to buy and sell, with low costs compared to physical real estate.

- Tied to long-term contracts (leases) that remain in place regardless of the economy, which keep their earnings resilient.

- More defensive in a recession since their cash flow is likely to be less affected than stocks.

However, you are still exposed to interest rate hikes affecting returns with REITs and REIT ETFs. As interest rates increase, the cost of borrowing increases, decreasing the distributions to shareholders. Furthermore, an S&P 500 index fund already provides plenty of diversification, some of which is real estate-related, and you can expect more reliable returns from an index fund. While some REITs have shown to have higher performance than index funds, historical records of the stock market go much further back than the stock market performance of REITs, providing a longer track record.

The question then is: Do you want real estate exposure without the costs associated with owning a property? If you do, then a REIT is a low-cost, easy way to have exposure to real estate. If you want to own a home, however, then make sure you do your homework.

10 FACTORS TO CONSIDER WHEN BUYING A HOME

This is not to say buying a home is a bad idea. Keep these 10 factors in mind when considering purchasing a home.

1.   Know How Much You Qualify For

Remember that the rule of thumb is not to spend more than a quarter of your take home pay on housing and less is better. More than that and your finances will be too tight, leaving you financially strained if things go wrong. If you want to retire early, aim for much less than 25%. Of course, this is not always possible, especially for expensive cities. Use mortgage calculators online to see how much your payments will be. It helps to talk to a bank first to get an idea of how much you will qualify for. Be careful because banks will qualify you for the maximum they feel you can afford, but that is a dangerous game. Rising interest rates could leave you with very little buffer in your finances.

If you want to save the most money while making mortgage payments, aim for a mortgage that is half what the banker or realtor tells you are qualified for, if possible. This depends on how much house you want to own and your personal circumstances. You might need a more expensive home for a large family, for example.

2.   Homes Are Long-Term

Homes are expensive. Between realtor fees, 3% to 6% when you buy and sell; closing costs, 2% to 5% of the purchase price, which include legal fees, inspections, title insurance, credit checks, and appraisals; and property taxes, chances are that breaking even will take at least five years of owning the property. Furthermore, for the first few years, your mortgage payments are mostly interest. Do not forget the cost of maintaining the property.

Because of the costs involved with real estate, only buy a house if you are planning to live in the same place long term. I own multiple properties with the intention of holding them for at least 10 years each. The longer you stay in your home, the more you save. Just like owning a car, the real savings happen over time. If you bought a house and find out you cannot live in the same place for that long, then you have the option of renting it out.

3. Do Not Be House Rich and Cash Poor

One common reason people do not have enough money to retire is that they become house rich and cash poor, meaning their home is their largest asset without much spare cash. As a result, many:

- Retire later than originally planned
- Accept a lower standard of living in retirement
- Move to a less expensive home and use the extra equity to fund their retirement
- Borrow against their home equity

Do not be one of those people. Stocks, over time, have always outperformed the housing market, so while a house is nice to have, do not overextend yourself on the mortgage and save the difference in index funds. Remember, your home is your home, whatever it is, and it is not a speculative investment. Furthermore, it is better to diversify your investments outside of having everything in one basket, i.e., your home.

Think about it this way. Even if your primary focus is paying your mortgage first, the bank only cares if the most recent payment was made. The moment you stop making payments, you lose credibility, your credit score decreases, and you could potentially lose the house. If you have liquid investments and an emergency fund, these can help in times of need.

4.   Have an Emergency Fund First

There is a reason why Chapter 4: Build a Small Emergency Fund comes before this chapter. You should have enough saved up in an emergency fund before thinking about taking on a mortgage. Unexpected life events can and *will* happen, so be prepared before you take on the biggest debt of your life.

5.   Pay Off Other Debts Before Getting a Mortgage

When you apply for a mortgage, the bank will ask about your other debt obligations. These include car payments, credit cards, lines of credit, student loans, and other real estate you may own. If the amount you want to borrow exceeds 43% of your income,[92] you will have a hard time getting a mortgage. Your debt-to-income ratio will be too high.

What is the debt-to-income ratio (DTI)? Simply add up all your monthly debt payments and divide them by your gross monthly income. Your gross monthly income is generally the amount of money you earn before taxes and other deductions are taken out.

For example, if you pay $1,200 a month in mortgage payments, another $200 for a car loan, and $400 in other debts, your monthly debt payments are $1,800. If your gross monthly income is $5,000, then your DTI ratio is 36%.

Monthly debts= $1,800

$1,200 (mortgage) + $200 (car) + $400 (other expenses)

Gross monthly income= $5,000

DTI ratio= $1,800 / $5,000= 36%

It is important not to be anywhere close to a 43% debt-to-income ratio when qualifying for a mortgage. Many people think if they can qualify at or close to 43%, then they should take on the mortgage. This is the wrong way of thinking. Have your debts under control first, and preferably be debt-free, before taking on a mortgage. And, reduce that ratio. As previously mentioned, most experts say mortgage payments should not exceed 25% of your gross income. I say you should try to get this under 20%.

Another ratio lenders look at is your PITI ratio: your Principal, Interest, Property Taxes, and Insurance to gross monthly income. This ratio should not exceed 28%. For example, if your gross monthly income is $5,000, your PITI should not exceed $1,400.

6. The Bigger the Down Payment, the Better

The average down payment size is $20,000 or 7.6% of the median sales price of $263,000. What is sad is that this is one of the highest average down payments since the year 2000.

This is not good enough. I recommend putting down at least 20% for your down payment.

Why? The more money you put down, the lower your monthly mortgage payment, and the less interest you pay over time. Suppose, for example, you have a mortgage of $100,000, and you are paying it back over 30 years. If you pay 5% interest rates, you must pay back the lender $100,000 and nearly the equivalent amount again in interest! If you put down a higher down payment, you will also likely qualify for a lower interest rate, which will save you money in the long run.

Another reason to put at least 20% down is that if you pay any less, you need private mortgage insurance (PMI) in the U.S. or mortgage default insurance (CMHC) in Canada, which is very expensive. In the U.S., the annual cost ranges from 0.38% to 1.03% of your home's value or more than $1,250 on a $250,000 home depending on the loan to value, borrower's credit score, and debt-to-income ratio. In Canada, the premium can be a total that is between and 2.8% and 4.0%. What is worse, in Canada, is that this is tacked onto the price of your home, so you will be paying interest on that amount over time, increasing the amount you owe even more. The worst part? The insurance does not protect you. Instead, it protects the lender and is a total waste of money.

In the U.S., a mortgage with PMI looks like this:[93]

Asking Price	$250,000			
Down Payment %	5%	10%	15%	20%
Down Payment $	$12,500	$25,000	$37,500	$50,000
Amortization Period*	30 years	30 years	25 years	25 years
Private Mortgage Insurance (PMI)**	0.88% or $2,078 per year	0.63% or $1,406 per year	0.38% or $797 per year	$0
Total Mortgage Required	$237,500	$225,000	$212,500	$200,000

*Most common loan type in the U.S.
**Any down payment that is less than 5% will have a 1.03% PMI rate.

In Canada, a mortgage with CMHC looks like this:

Asking Price	$250,000			
Down Payment %	5%	10%	15%	20%
Down Payment $	$12,500	$25,000	$37,500	$50,000
Amortization Period*	25 years	25 years	25 years	25 years

	4% or $9,500	3.1% or $6,975	2.8% or $5,950	$0
Mortgage Default Insurance (CMHC)	4% or $9,500	3.1% or $6,975	2.8% or $5,950	$0
Total Mortgage Required	$247,000	$231,975	$218,450	$200,000

Note that in Canada, the mortgage default insurance is not available on homes purchased for more than $1,000,000. This means that a down payment of 20% is required on these homes. Also note, that the maximum amortization for insured mortgages is 25 years in Canada.

Why does the bank require you to have insurance if you have less than 20% of a down payment? It is because lenders believe that people who put down less than 20% are more likely to default.

7. Location, Location, Location

If you commute to work, put a dollar value on how much your free time is worth and do the math to see how much your commute time costs you. It has been proven that if you live close to work, you will be happier and healthier.[94] Americans on average spend more than 100 hours per year commuting to work, which is more than the two weeks of vacation that most workers take annually! People with the longest commutes have the lowest overall satisfaction in life. This is because time is limited and spending it on a commute makes us feel stressed. In fact, the daily commute is the number two activity people hate most on a day-to-day basis. The number one is housework. Cutting out a one-hour commute produces the happiness equivalent of a $40,000 raise. This is not to say that no commute is the best commute. Studies show that about a 15-minute commute is the ideal length, with walking being the best form of transportation.

For example, if you commute an hour to and from work each day and your hourly rate at work is $25 an hour, you spend the equivalent of $1,000 a month of time or losing $12,000 a year in traffic.

Not only will living closer to work make you happier, but it also costs less to maintain a car, and smaller homes closer to downtown tend to appreciate faster than larger homes farther away from the city.[95]

8. Buy a Primary Residence Before an Investment Property

Popular advice is to buy an investment property first to get your foot in the door, and then use the equity to buy your first family home in five years. This is terrible advice. Due to the upfront and ongoing costs of owning a home, buying an investment property first will eat into your savings and delay you getting into your own home.

9. Shop for Your Mortgage

Interest rates make an enormous difference in your monthly payments. Even a 0.25% difference between two rates can mean the difference of $32 a month or $1,920 over a five-year period. In the U.S., look up rates using Bankrate.com, HSH.com, and Zillow.com. In Canada, I recommend RateHub.ca.

If your mortgage is up for renewal or interest rates have recently dropped, look around for the best rate and negotiate with your bank. The best way to do this is to see if there is a rate that is lower than your current rate. If so, call up your bank, and ask for the "customer retention department," and use this script:

"Hello, I've been a long-time customer, but I'm thinking of switching my mortgage to another bank, which has this offer. Given our long relationship, I'd rather continue my business with you. So, would you be able to match the offer? If not, please send me the forms so that I can switch."

Whether you are actually willing to switch banks does not matter. See what they come back with. If they say that they cannot match the rate, ask to speak with their supervisor and see what deal they can offer. Let's say you save 0.5% from doing this with a five-year fixed rate, going from 2.99% to 2.49%. That 10-minute phone call would save you $1,412 a year and $7,059 over five years.

Tax Tips

In the U.S., you can deduct mortgage interest from your income to reduce your taxes for the year. Note that tax law changes in 2018 put limitations on this. This is an additional bonus whether you use the home as your principal residence or rental property.

In Canada, you can only deduct mortgage interest if the house is a rental property. This means that you rent it out to a tenant. You cannot deduct mortgage interest from your principal residence to reduce your income.

Under no circumstance, in the U.S. or Canada, can you use the principal repayments as a tax deduction.

10. Go with a Fixed Rate Mortgage

Almost always lock in a fixed rate. A fixed-rate mortgage is a mortgage where the interest rate on the loan remains the same throughout the term of the loan. The most common term is usually either for 25 or 30 years, but you can get less. In Canada, they have 1 to 10-year renewal periods, and in either country, you can refinance your mortgage if rates decrease. It is harder, however, to lock in a lower rate when rates have increased. Getting a fixed rate in these circumstances gives you peace of mind and allows you to budget the rest of your income without needing to worry about increasing interest rates.

The other option is a variable-rate mortgage. In the U.S., it is also referred to as an adjustable-rate mortgage (ARM). The interest rates on a variable-rate mortgage fluctuate depending on what happens to the interest rates in the economy, which is decided by the Federal Reserve or Bank of Canada. When you hear "rate hikes" on the news, it refers to this interest rate. Typically, a variable-rate mortgage has lower rates than a fixed-rate, but whether it remains low is uncertain. And if rates rise when the economy is doing well, which is what usually happens, you will soon wish you locked in your rate at the fixed rate.

OTHER MORTGAGE CONSIDERATIONS

Open or Closed Mortgage?[96]

Open Mortgages Provide More Flexibility

With open mortgages, the entire mortgage balance can be paid off at any time without penalty. But open mortgage rates are usually variable rates and are a little higher than closed rates. You will likely pay the prime rate plus a hefty premium.

Fortunately, open mortgages allow you to move into a fixed-rate mortgage at any time if you feel that variable rates are going to go up. The freedom to pay them off or move to another product at any time is a major selling point for open mortgages.

Closed Mortgages Offer Attractive Interest Rates

Closed mortgages typically have lower interest rates than open mortgages, but borrowers have limited flexibility. For example, you cannot pay off the loan without incurring a penalty. However, most closed mortgages allow for accelerated payments of some kind. Each lender has its own prepayment terms.

With a closed mortgage, you agree to keep the loan for the entire term. Borrowers who sell their house early into the term because of relocation or job loss can end up with less money than they anticipated because the high penalties eat into their equity. If this happens to you, I highly recommend trying to rent out your place first until the end of the term.

Should you go with an open or closed mortgage? It depends on your current financial situation and what you expect your financial situation to be in the future. Essentially, you pay a higher rate to have more flexibility with an open mortgage. My advice? Go with the closed mortgage. Only buy a property if you plan on owning it long term, ideally 10 years or more. And, the interest savings will be tens of thousands of dollars over that time. If you find your financial situation changes or you get a job elsewhere, rent the home out until the end of the term and then sell. Note that both fixed-rate and variable-rate mortgages can be either open or closed mortgages.

Prepayment Penalty Fees

With either variable- or fixed-rate mortgages, there is typically a fee associated with selling your property before the end of the term, assuming you have a closed mortgage.[97] This fee is referred to as the mortgage prepayment penalty.

In the U.S., the amount of the mortgage prepayment penalty varies from bank to bank. Typically, they fall under the following types for fixed-rate mortgages:[98]

- Fixed, flat fee,
- Percentage of the owed interest,
- Percentage of the remaining balance, or
- Sliding scale.

For example, some lenders may charge penalties such as 80% of six months of interest on your final loan balance, while others will calculate between 2% and 5% of the balance itself.

In Canada, the mortgage prepayment penalty for fixed-rate mortgages is the greater of:

- Three months of interest or
- The interest rate differential (IRD).

Three months of interest is the amount of interest you would have paid in a three-month period on your current mortgage.

The interest rate differential is a little trickier. This is your lender's way of determining how much interest they will lose by letting you break your contract early, and then making you pay the interest to them. To calculate the IRD, your lender looks at your mortgage rate, how much time is left in your mortgage term, and the mortgage rate they could charge someone now for a new term equal to the remainder of your term. It can be worse. Many banks use the posted rate at the time you received your mortgage versus the actual negotiated rate you received to determine the difference, which makes the differential even larger.

For example, let's say you received 3.89% on your five-year fixed rate, have 24 months left in your contract, and $250,000 outstanding on your mortgage. Depending on the bank, they would look at what the posted rate was for a five-year rate the day you originally signed your contract with them. For this example, we use 5.49%. Then, the bank would find out what product would cover the remainder of your term. In this case, it would be a two-year fixed-rate mortgage, and let's say the posted rate is 3.14%.

IRD=

(5.49% posted rate at original mortgage date − 3.14% posted rate for remaining term) / 12 months= 0.0020 IRD Factor

0.0020 IRD Factor x $250,000 x 24 months remaining = $12,000

For variable-rate mortgages, the penalty in Canada is three months of interest. As previously stated, a variable-rate mortgage typically has lower rates than a fixed-rate mortgage.

For example, let's say your interest rate is 2.50%, and you need to break your mortgage early.

Mortgage prepayment penalty fee=

2.50% your existing mortgage rate x $250,000 / 12 months
x 3 months= $1,563

As you see, the mortgage prepayment penalty can be large. So, this is another reason to hold real estate for long periods and only look to sell when nearing the end of the term.

Making Early Payments

If interest on your mortgage is low, then it makes sense to borrow money in the form of a mortgage. While this statement is generally true, many people use this argument as justification to spend more money in other areas of their life rather than save and invest. Some people I know use low interest rates to buy brand new cars and live on high-cost lifestyles supplied by cheap debt. Their investments, on the other hand, are small in comparison. These people are better off paying down their mortgage, rather than buying the latest iPhone, because they are using the leverage afforded by the mortgage to purchase liabilities rather than assets.

The same reasoning applies if interest rates increase. As rates increase, you save more interest over time if you make additional payments. For example, if you have a 25-year $250,000 mortgage at an interest rate of 5% and make an additional $100 per month in payments, you shorten your mortgage by 2.9 years, saving $25,009 in interest. If you make an additional $200 per month in payments, you shorten your mortgage by 5.2 years, saving $43,800 in interest.

Assuming a $250,000 Mortgage at 5% Interest

Additional Monthly Payment	Total Interest Savings	Mortgage Shortens by
$50	$13,471	1.5 years
$100	$25,009	2.9 years
$200	$43,800	5.2 years
$300	$58,499	7 years

If you make $0 in additional payments, you end up paying $436,204 over the course of 25 years.

Total payment= $250,000 + $186,204 interest= $436,204

If this was an adjustable-rate mortgage, there could be a risk that rates rise over the 25-year period, costing the purchaser even more in interest if they do not make additional payments. While the stock market would return more over the same time, do not discount the savings attributed to making payments early, especially if you find it hard to save money outside of your mortgage.

Using Leverage to Your Advantage

You can make a lot of money by carrying a mortgage balance on your rental houses rather than buying them with cash. For simplicity's sake, say they cost $125,000 each, and you have $125,000 to invest. You can put down 20% down on five houses ($25,000 each x 5 = $125,000) or 100% down on one ($125,000 x 1 = $125,000). Let's say rent in the area is $1,500 per month. If you buy rental properties and use the 50% rule, which is a conservative rule of thumb, that assumes 50% of your rental income goes toward operating costs of the property, such as taxes, repairs, and property and management fees.

Scenario 1: Pay $125,000 cash for one property

- Monthly cash flow: $1,500
- 50% Rule: $1,500 x 50%= $750 for expenses
- Net monthly cash flow: $1,500 - $750= $750
- Yearly net cash flow: $750 x 12= $9,000

Scenario 2: Pay 20% down or $25,000 each for 5 properties

- Monthly cash flow: $1,500 x 5 units= $7,500
- 50% Rule: $1,500 x 50% x 5 units= $3,750 for expenses
- Monthly interest cost at 5%= $390 x 5 units= $1,950
- Net monthly cash flow: $3,750 - $1,950= $1,800
- Yearly net cash flow $1,800 x 12 = $21,600

You make more than 2x your cash flow using Scenario 2. And, this assumes no price appreciation. On top of that, for rental properties you can write off your interest in both Canada and the U.S. Plus, you can also deduct depreciation from the income you make from your property, resulting in fewer taxes owed on the income earned.

Why not just invest in real estate then? Again, appreciation is not guaranteed. Furthermore, it depends on a person's risk tolerance. Could you sleep at night knowing you owed $375,000 across five properties? What if they are not occupied? Moreover, it is hard to find a property that fits the 50% rule. If you cannot find a property that meets the criteria, or at the very least has a positive cash flow, then rental properties are not recommended. Lastly, the fees associated with buying and selling are a hindrance to your long-term success, so only dive into real estate investing only if you have a long-term outlook.

HOME EQUITY LINE OF CREDIT (HELOC)

A Home Equity Line of Credit (HELOC)[99] is a revolving loan funded by your home's equity, previously known as a second mortgage, and often tied to a bank account or credit card. Many banks give you a line of credit equal to about 80% of your equity.

So, the owner of a $200,000 house, with $50,000 paid off, will have access to a $40,000 home equity line of credit. Often people use a HELOC to consolidate their high-interest debt, make home renovations, or pay for schooling for their children. Sounds great on paper, but using your house as collateral when you have worked hard to pay back your mortgage is not recommended unless you are in a good financial position.

Five reasons to avoid a HELOC:[100]

1. **Miss payments, and you can lose your home.** While it may make sense to consolidate your high-interest credit card debt with your low-interest HELOC, you could potentially lose your home if something comes up and you cannot make the payment. If you miss a credit card payment, you may be exposed to fees and a decrease in your credit rating, but you will not lose your house.

2. **It is not a dependable emergency fund.** Banks can freeze your HELOC at any time if your credit rating drops.

3. **They are variable rates.** HELOCs are appealing because of the low interest rates, but if interest rates increase, then your debt costs increase as well. As a result, you could have a five-year fixed rate mortgage combined with a variable-rate HELOC, which adds uncertainty to debt management. Some HELOCs are available with a fixed-rate option, which may be a better choice.

4. **HELOCs may require a balloon repayment**. This means that you pay back all the money owed at the end of a predetermined period. If finances are tight, then making this payment could be difficult.

5. **You may not be able to refinance without paying your HELOC first**. If you want to refinance your mortgage because rates have decreased, you may have to pay back your HELOC first.

If you have no debt, an emergency fund, and built up investments, then using a HELOC as springy debt to complement your emergency fund can make sense as long you do not use it as your initial source of liquidity. And, always keep it at a zero balance.

SUMMARY

If decide you would rather buy a home than rent and have done your research, then follow this checklist:

1. Have all debts paid off first and your emergency fund established.

2. Real estate is long-term. Otherwise, it is a poor investment. Keep a property for a minimum of five years and preferably 10.

3. Do not be house rich and cash poor. Focus on investing excess savings in index fund ETFs.

4. The bigger the down payment, the better.

5. Use online calculators to determine what mortgage payment you can afford comfortably. Keep it under 25%, preferably under 20%, of your gross income.

6. Shop around for rates using sites like bankrate.com and ratehub.ca.

7. Consider what you really want in a house and stay consistent.

8. Get prequalified by a bank.

9. Remember, location, location, location.

10. Only use home equity lines of credit if you are in a good financial position and as springy debt to complement your emergency fund.

PART FOUR

LIVING YOUR LIFE

This final part of the book focuses on two aspects: Retirement and Happiness. In Chapter 13: Find a Purpose in Retirement, I talk about finding a purpose in retirement. The goal in retirement should be to have enough money so that you can live comfortably without needing to work AND do what you have always wanted but never had the time for. Maybe you would like to volunteer more, travel, or make a legacy for your children. Whatever it may be, too many people strive only for the financial goal and once achieved, retire without having made future plans. Over time, they become restless and depressed. Instead, decide before you retire what you want to do and create those goals in advance. It will help drive you and keep you motivated to meet your financial goals. It will also be a far more rewarding and exciting time once you are retired.

In Chapter 14: Happiness, I end the book by providing ways to lead a happier and more fulfilling life so that you can live to your utmost potential. You have one life, so enjoy it! Live your life the way you want to experience it. Remember, early retirement does not mean the end of your working career but instead means being the *best* version of yourself. You will finally have the time to concentrate on what you really want to do. The tips in this book are meant to provide a way for you to achieve that, without sacrificing your quality of life or happiness on the road to get there.

CHAPTER THIRTEEN

FIND A PURPOSE IN RETIREMENT

FILLING THE VOID

The concept of retirement is unique to the past five decades. Not too long ago, the average American had two stages of life—work and death. Today, the average American retires at age 62. Compare this with 100 years ago when the average American died at age 51. People are now living longer, well into their retirement years.

The biggest questions then become:

- How are you going to achieve a sense of accomplishment and satisfaction without going to work?

- How will you be able to relate to your friends and family if you retire before they do?

- If you retire early, who will you spend your time with?

For most people, the novelty of retirement wears off after a month or two. You may start to feel that you no longer have a reason to wake up in the morning. Once you do get up, you may feel you have nowhere to go. There is no more socializing in the office, no more going for coffee, no more people stopping by your desk, no more clients, and no more challenges to give your life purpose.

Much of the Western world misperceives what contributes to a happy and fulfilling retirement. Many people have grand ideas of how great and wonderful life in retirement will be. These ideas can include no more daily commute, no more dealing with a boss, always traveling, sleeping in, and doing what you want when you want.

Retirement can be many things. For some, it is living their fantasy, for others it is disappointing, and for yet others, it is a struggle. In fact, for many, the reality is the opposite of their fantasy. This is especially true for those with few interests outside of work. According to a study by the London-based Institute of Economic Affairs, depression risk increases by 40% after retiring.[101]

Many save for 40 years to build a retirement nest egg but are unprepared when the time comes. People focus only on the financial aspect of retirement, forgetting to consider the other factors.

Work fills four unique voids in our lives:

1. Sense of Community

Our social connections are the single largest driver of our happiness. New York Times bestselling author Daniel Gilbert writes in *Stumbling on Happiness*, "If I wanted to predict your happiness and I could only know one thing about you, I wouldn't want to know about your gender, religion, health, or income. I'd want to know about the strength of your relationships with your friends and family."

You may not miss your workplace when you retire, but you will likely miss the people you work with. Social interaction makes life more enjoyable for most of us. Many people get their only companionship from work. They lose the skill to develop new friendships outside of the workplace. To feel part of a community, individuals must put in the effort to be active in the community, whether through volunteering or being part of a club. A sense of community translates into social, emotional, and physical well-being. Research shows that people who have intimate relationships with others live happier, healthier, and longer. Those who are lonely stand a greater chance of dying an early death. Former U.S. President Jimmy Carter said:

"There are two basic secrets to successful aging: one is staying active in doing things that we find interesting. And the other one is having an intimate relationship with other human beings, so we don't just become a vegetable sitting in front of a flickering TV screen and depending on other people to do things for us that we are capable of doing ourselves."

A sense of community can have more of an impact on the quality of your retirement than good health and finances.

2. Structure

Most of us believe that we are supposed to be working continually throughout our adult lives, for no other reason than to fill the hours between 8 am and 5 pm with some structured activity. Working at something that you dislike, even if it has no other purpose, provides routine and structure in our lives that we derive comfort from.

3. Stimulation

Work gives us a setting to learn and discover new things about the world and other people. There are many diverse perspectives and personalities that you would never encounter elsewhere. Retiring in the traditional sense removes a primary source of stimulation from our lives.

4. Purpose

Many of us give so much to our jobs that we do not have the time or energy to develop other interests. Work is the primary source of identity for many of us and where we put most of our energy and creativity. To lose work means losing our identity. This is arguably the most important void that needs filling when we retire. Once we have a purpose, everything else falls into place.

FINDING A PURPOSE

Pasricha writes in the *Happiness Equation* that men and women in Okinawa live an average of seven years longer than Americans and have the longest disability-free life expectancy on Earth. Researchers from *National Geographic* were so intrigued by this phenomenon that they studied Okinawa residents in search of the reason for their longevity. The key finding? Okinawans do not "retire" like Americans do, living life on the golf course, sitting around on cottage docks, and staring at the clouds. No, they do not even have the word retire in their vocabulary. What they do have is called "ikigai," which translates to "the reason you wake up in the morning."

Ikigai is the reason you find people over the age of 100 in Okinawa: Teaching their craft to students, practicing martial arts, fishing, or hanging around with their great-great-great-granddaughter. Researchers at Tohoku University took the study a step further. They spent seven years in Sendai, Japan, studying over 43,000 Japanese by asking them the question, "Do you have an ikigai in your life?"

At the end of the study, they found that those who reported having an ikigai were more likely to be married, educated, and have a job. They were healthier overall and had lower levels of stress. Furthermore, 95% of them were still alive after the study. Only 83% of those without an ikigai made it that long.

Find your ikigai.

Helping You Find a Purpose

It can be hard to determine what your purpose should be. Use this list to get started:

- Go back to university or college or take online courses that interest you.

- Learn a new language.
- Create a bucket list of places you want to travel to and do it. Take time to experience the culture and customs of each country and talk to the locals.
- Volunteer with an organization.
- Help the underprivileged.
- Write a book.
- Practice public speaking.
- Pursue a side hustle or spend more time on one you already have.
- Help others achieve retirement.
- Give yourself athletic goals like running a marathon, weightlifting, or enroll in a martial arts program.
- Create a list of books you want to read. Reading all the classics is a great goal.
- Learn how to dance.
- Start a blog.
- Set family goals. Decide what kind of parent or partner you want to be.
- Conquer a fear you have.
- Start meditating.
- Learn to cook.

Setting Goals

When finding a purpose for your life, there is a difference between goal setting and goal achievement. Both are important, but setting goals is not enough. You need to achieve them. If you feel blocked, Tim Ferriss recommends writing down the following:

- One place to visit
- One thing to do before you die (a memory of a lifetime)

- One thing to do daily
- One thing to do weekly
- One thing you have always wanted to learn

Set short-term and long-term goals. Write down a specific goal with a specific deadline. If the goal is five years away, set short-term goals you can achieve while working toward the long-term goal.

For example, say your goal is running a marathon one year from today. Your short-term goals could be to run once a week for the first month, then twice a week, then a certain distance, and then a distance per month.

Develop a system where you create little steps on a regular basis that move you toward your desired result. Scott Adams in his book *How to Fail at Almost Everything and Still Win Big* calls this process "creating systems."

"Goal-oriented people exist in a state of continuous pre-success failure at best, and permanent failure at worst if things never work out. Systems people succeed every time they apply their systems, in the sense that they did what they intended to do. The goals people are fighting the feeling of discouragement at each turn. The systems people are feeling good every time they apply their system. That's a big difference in terms of maintaining your personal energy in the right direction."

In the same vein, Tim Ferriss says the key is to set easily attainable goals that you can over deliver on. "Alleviating that performance anxiety... allows you to overshoot that goal, continually succeed, and sort of build that confidence and momentum." He continues, "The feeling that you're winning, is a precursor to winning on a really large scale."

You want to set realistic goals to avoid putting too much pressure on yourself, giving you the option of smashing them out of the park. If the goals are not realistic and you have no plan of attack for accomplishing them, then they are inflexible goals and can set you up for disappointment.

Here is an example of creating inflexible goals versus systems:

Inflexible Goals

- Lose 20 pounds in one year.
- Write a 200-page book.

Systems

- Be active every day: Could be to walk up the stairs instead of the elevator or walk to work.
- Write every day: Could be for 10 minutes, one hour, or more.

Inflexible goals set you up for disappointment if you do not fulfill them. The systems, however, make it easier to win daily.

Whether you call setting small goal systems or refer to them as realistic goals, they are the same concept.

Another key is not to set too many. It is okay to set a couple, achieve them, and then set more. And, I know what you are probably thinking, "In Chapter 1, he said that I should be content with what I have, so why am I setting goals?"

You can set ambitious goals while at the same time being content and satisfied. How? It is all about whether your goals are intrinsic or extrinsic. If you set goals to impress other people or to gain status, money, or power, those are extrinsic goals. In this case, you will be running on the "hedonic treadmill" I mentioned in Chapter 1: Be More with Less, always trying for more, never satisfied, and never happy. If your goals are intrinsic, however, such as setting a goal because you want to learn something new to become a better person, you can be both goal-oriented and satisfied at the same time. Do things that will make you happy.

GET OVER YOUR FEARS

A lot of retirees think that they will finally do what they want to do in retirement, believing that they will finally have the time they need. Then, when they retire, they find they are afraid to take action. If you are nervous about starting something new or simply putting it off because you fear the unknown, try this solution. Tim Ferriss refers to this as "Fear Setting":

1. **Define your worst-case scenario.** Write out every detail and rate it on a scale of 1 to 10 of how bad the outcome could be. How likely is this to occur? Are the results somehow permanent?

2. **What steps could you take to undo the damage or get things back on track, even temporarily?** It is likely easier than you think.

3. **What are the outcomes or benefits, both temporary and permanent, of more likely scenarios?** Now that you wrote down the worst-case scenario, what is the more probable scenario? What would the impact of these be on a scale of 1 to 10? What is the more moderately good outcome and how likely is that?

4. **If you retired today, what would you do to get things under financial control?** This is to help you think through what is putting you off from retiring.

5. **What are you putting off out of fear?** Usually, what we fear most is what we most need to do. The fear of not knowing the outcome is what prevents us from doing what we need to do.

6. **What is it costing you—financially, emotionally, and physically—to postpone action?** Do not simply assess the cost of taking action. It is equally important to measure the downside of the cost of inaction. If you do

not pursue those things that excite you, where will you be one year into retirement, five years, ten years? Inaction is the greatest risk of all.

7. **What are you waiting for?** Chances are you cannot answer this with any legitimate argument. The answer is simple: You are afraid just like most people. Measure the cost of inaction, realize the unlikelihood of the worst-case scenario and reparability of most missteps, and develop the most important habit of those who are happy in retirement: Action.

SUMMARY

People are living longer than ever into their retirement years. Focusing on the financial side of retirement is important, but just as valuable is planning for what you want to do once you retire, especially if you retire at a younger age. To get started, follow this advice:

- **Ask yourself questions to find what you want to do in retirement.** Look for activities that will provide you with a sense of community, structure, offer stimulation, and a sense of purpose. If you find a sense of purpose, everything else will fall into place. Figuring out what you want to do in retirement makes retiring far easier.

- **Stay active, set realistic goals, and create systems to achieve them every day.** You can never be too young to retire if you have saved 25x your annual expenditures.

- **Practice fear setting**. A lot of people living in retirement are afraid of taking action. It allows you to visualize all the bad things that could happen to you and the steps you can take to mitigate them. You will often find that the worst thing that can happen is not as bad as first imagined when you have a plan.

CHAPTER FOURTEEN

HAPPINESS

Happiness comes from meeting certain core human needs. The thing is there are many ways to meet each of those wants—some cheap, some free, and some expensive. For example, travel is a great way to experience new things and get outside of your comfort zone. But you can accomplish this by staying in $50-a-night hostels, $200-a-night hotels, or $1,000-a-night luxury hotels. Same happiness, different cost. The same holds true for most things in life. Almost everything is available at a wide range of costs. It is up to you to decide what makes you happy and spend appropriately. So, live your life the way you want to live it because you only live once.

Explore the following for a better chance at a good life and greater happiness:

1. **Focus on your physical health.** If you are not healthy, then everything else you do will bring less joy.

    - Exercise regularly. Not only will you look good, but you will also feel good. Tony Robbins says, "motion equals emotion." Even a 7-minute workout to start your day will make you feel better. I make it a habit of working out every day at lunch and then reward myself with a sweet. Remember the habit loop: cue – routine – reward.

    - Eat a healthy diet. You will have more energy during the day and feel better about yourself. I meal prep on Sundays, so I know exactly what I am eating throughout the week.

    - Get enough sleep. Jeff Bezos, CEO of Amazon, makes getting eight hours of sleep a night a priority.

- Drink enough water, at least eight glasses per day. Studies[102] show that hydration has a major effect on energy levels and brain function. I fill up my 34-ounce water bottle first thing in the morning and refill it at lunch.

- Get outside more. Spending time in the fresh air has been shown to increase happiness. I love running outside and going for hikes.

2. **Focus on your mental health**. Practice meditation, mindfulness, and gratitude daily. I meditate at least 15 minutes every morning as soon as I get up and use the 5 Minute Journal to practice gratitude. Practicing mindfulness is one of the most important things you can do, and top performers cannot recommend it enough.

   - Tim Ferriss on his podcast, The Tim Ferriss Show, found that over 80% of his guests have some form of meditation practice.

   - Tony Robbins channels his energy with a 9-minute priming exercise every morning. He breaks it down into three-minute sections:

     1. Think of three things you are grateful for.

     2. Focus on creating gratitude by imagining an inner presence that can heal and solve any obstacles in your life.

     3. Identify three things you are absolutely going to make happen for yourself. Imagine what it would feel like to complete these tasks and "see it as though it's already been done."

3. **Learn constantly.** Challenge yourself every day to learn something new, whether a new language or how to dance. You want to continuously learn. I read at least 20 pages of a book each day, in addition to listening to 20

minutes of either a podcast or audiobook on my walk to work. Keep your mind active. Other suggestions include:

- Take a painting class
- Learn a new language
- Learn to program
- Start a website
- Join a book club

4. **Solve problems.** Part of the happiness equation is changing your reality. We need something to accomplish. To do this, solve problems. Happiness is a work in progress because solving problems is a work in progress.

   - Set goals. This is the best way to set your mind to something and achieve it. Make them daily and often, leading up to a larger goal. Once accomplished, set another and then another.

5. **Indulge and splurge, in moderation.** I am not perfect and do not follow everything in this book 100%. While I stand behind everything I have written and follow it most days, I splurge and treat myself in moderation. Have fun and enjoy life! You have one life to live.

6. **Travel.** One of the best methods to find a purpose is to travel. You are exposed to new people, cultures, and lifestyles. You gain valuable insights and ways of seeing the world, which can give you a new purpose.

   - Look for flight deals using apps like Hopper or Kayak. If you live in Canada, look up flight deals using your airport code and adding deals, like yyzdeals.com or yycdeals.com. I flew roundtrip to Peru for $480 a few years ago.

7. **Do one thing per day that scares you.** By breaking out of your comfort zone, you gain confidence, and over time, your comfort zone will expand so much that your small sphere of comfort will turn into a large circle.

   - Afraid of swimming? Take swimming classes.
   - Afraid of talking to strangers? Strike up a conversation with at least one random person per day.
   - Afraid of heights? Sign up for a skydiving class.

8. **Spend time with your family and friends.** Close relationships are a key to happiness. Studies show that social time is highly valuable for improving our happiness even for introverts, and losing touch with family and friends is one of the top five regrets of the dying. If you find you are losing touch with people you care about, try the following:

   - Create a list of people you want to keep in touch with.
   - Set reminders when you want to reach out.
   - Invite them to coffee or some other activity to hang out. If they turn you down or forget to reply, follow up again after. People are usually busy, and it is up to you to make the first move.

9. **Volunteer.** Volunteering gives us a greater purpose in life and helping others is tremendously rewarding. Even as little as two hours a week is ideal to enrich our lives. For me, I teach high school students how to start a business with Junior Achievement's Company Program and am a Global Shaper as part of the World Economic Forum. A volunteer position exists for almost anything you can think of. The more personal the cause is to you, the more rewarding you will find it.

10. **Move closer to work.** A short commute is worth more than a big house. A commute can have a significant impact on your happiness.

This book, backed by science and human psychology, is a system of living your best life in **all ways** rather than saving every dollar. I do not advocate living without but rather living life to the fullest. Everything I wrote will not apply to you, so use what works for *you*. There is no right or wrong way to incorporate the ideas in this book, and they are always open for tweaking. Whatever you take away is yours to keep. In fact, I challenge you to refine and adapt the ideas to make them your own and to fit your life. If you believe in yourself and your capabilities, you can achieve anything.

Lastly, I end by asking you to take the time to appreciate life. When you walk down the street, stop and smell the flowers. Often, the small things in life are the big things. Focusing too much on the larger picture of early retirement can take the fun out of day-to-day living—that is not what I want for anyone. Be frugal but not cheap. Take up a side hustle that interests you. Invest wisely in index funds. And, set your finances in a way that is automatic so that you can spend time on the things that bring you joy. By following the advice in this book, early retirement is a bonus.

ACKNOWLEDGEMENTS

When I pick up a book for the first time, I like to flip to the Acknowledgements. Like many readers, I'm eager to see where the author got their inspiration and who helped them get their book to where it is today. This book has been a long time in the making so I want to give credit to those who helped me along the way. If I miss anyone, I apologize; any omissions are inadvertent.

First and foremost, I want to thank my editors, Samantha Mason, who improved my writing and encouraged me to get this book out into the world into as many hands as possible, and Fraser Nelund, who was patient revising my first draft. I will forever be grateful. I also want to thank my friends and family who helped improve my earlier drafts. For their invaluable comments, I thank Ryan Cramer, Judy Ferris, Lina Kudzhak, Dalia Nasr, Kourtney Rylands, Melissa Ta, and Leo Tam.

I am immensely grateful for everyone who had faith in me and supported me. All those long evenings and weekends certainly took its toll but your understanding and commitment will not be forgotten. And finally, for this book's beautiful cover, I am grateful to my graphic designer, Mila, and also Sue Balcer for doing the interior design work.

ABOUT THE AUTHOR

Chris Dumont is the founder of MoneySensei.com, a personal finance hub that offers a blog and e-courses to help guide people to become financially free.

For nearly a decade, he has worked in finance learning both inside and outside the classroom the fundamentals of personal finance. Chris holds an MBA from the Schulich School of Business in Toronto, Ontario and a Bachelor of Commerce from the Alberta School of Business with a major in Finance. He completed his CFA designation in 2016.

Chris lives in Calgary, Alberta, Canada where he is often found running in Eau Claire, petting as many dogs as he comes across.

Connect with Chris:

Blog:	moneysensei.com
LinkedIn:	Chris Dumont
Facebook:	@themoneysensei
Twitter:	@moneysensei_
Instagram:	@moneysensei_

Notes

1       $3.82 trillion divided by US population estimate https://www.census.gov/pop-clock/

2   David Clingingsmith, "Negative emotions, income, and welfare: Causal estimates from the PSID," *Journal of Economic Behavior & Organization*, Elsevier, vol. 130(C), 1-19.

3   Daniel T. Gilbert, and Timothy D. Wilson, "Affective forecasting knowing what to want," *Current Directions in Psychological Science*, 14 (3), (June 2015): 131-134.

4   Raksha Arora, Ed Diener, and James K. Harter, Weiting Ng, "Wealth and happiness across the world," Journal of Personality and Social Psychology, 99 (1): 52-61.

5   Philip Brickman, Dan Coates, and Ronnie Janoff-Bulman, "Lottery winners and accident victims: Is happiness relative?" *Journal of Personality and Social Psychology*, 36 (8): 917.

6   Bart Duriez, Joke Simons, Bart Soenens, and Maarten Vansteenkiste, "Materialistic Values and Well-Being Among Business Students: Further Evidence of Their Detrimental Effect, *Journal of Applied Social Psychology*, 36 (12): 2892-2908.

7   Bronnie Ware, *The Top Five Regrets of the Dying: A Life Transformed by the Dearly Departed* (Hay House Inc., 2012).

8   Tim Ferriss, "Managing Procrastination, Predicting the Future, and Finding Happiness," *The Tim Ferriss Show*, November 30, 2017.

9   Faisal Hoque, "Why extremely successful people swear by this 5-minute daily habit," accessed August 6, 2018, http://www.businessinsider.com/why-extremely-successful-people-swear-by-this-5-minute-daily-habit-2015-11.

10   Robert Emmons, *Thanks!: How the Science of Gratitude Can Make You Happier* (Mariner Books, 2008).

11   "Wealth, Asset Ownership, & Debt of Households Detailed Tables: 2013," United States Census Bureau, accessed August 6, 2018, https://www.census.gov/data/tables/2013/demo/wealth/wealth-asset-ownership.html.

12   Assuming 9.7% annual returns with an S&P 500 index fund

13   Walecia Konrad, "How to Manage Dental Costs, With or Without Insurance," New York Times, accessed August 6, 2018, https://www.nytimes.com/2009/09/05/health/05patient.html.

14   Agota Bialobzeksky, "The Science of Self-Control: Can You Increase Your Willpower?" Pick the Brain, accessed August 6, 2018, http://www.pickthebrain.com/blog/the-science-of-self-control-can-you-increase-your-willpower/.

15   * William Bengen first articulated the 4% rule, but the Trinity study popularized the idea

16   Assuming an 5% rate of return on your savings and 4% withdrawal rate

17   "The Shockingly Simple Math Behind Early Retirement," Mr. Money Mustache, accessed August 6, 2018, http://www.mrmoneymustache.com/2012/01/13/the-shockingly-simple-math-behind-early-retirement/

18   "California Dentist Salaries," Salary.com, accessed August 6, 2018, https://www1.salary.com/CA/Dentist-salary.html.

19   "California Receptionist Salaries," Salary.com, accessed August 6, 2018, https://www1.salary.com/CA/Receptionist-salary.html.

20   Tanza Loudenback, "Middle-class America made more money last year than ever before," accessed August 6, 2018, http://www.businessinsider.com/us-census-median-income-2017-9.

21   Editors of Kiplinger's Personal Finance Magazine, "9 Reasons You Need an Emergency Fund," accessed August 6, 2018, https://www.neamb.com/finance/9-reasons-you-need-an-emergency-fund.htm.

22   Robert Digiacomo, "Is Dental Insurance Worth the Cost?" Bankrate, accessed August 6, 2018, https://www.bankrate.com/finance/insurance/dental-insurance-1.aspx.

23   "Interest and penalties," Government of Canada, accessed August 6, 2018, https://www.canada.ca/en/revenue-agency/services/tax/individuals/topics/about-your-tax-return/interest-penalties.html.

24   "Personal Accounts Interest Rates," Banking Accounts & Services, RBC, accessed August 6, 2018, http://www.rbcroyalbank.com/rates/persacct.html#daysavings.

25   Martha C. White, "Here's How Long It Really Takes to Get a Job," Money, accessed August 6, 2018, http://time.com/money/4053899/how-long-it-takes-to-get-hired/.

26   Claire Tsosie, "What Happens If I Make Only the Minimum Payment on my Credit Card?" NerdWallet, accessed August 6, 2018, https://www.nerdwallet.com/blog/credit-cards/minimum-payment-credit-card/.

27   "Credit Card Terms," Minimum payment, RBC, accessed August 6, 2018, http://www.rbcroyalbank.com/credit-cards/managing_credit/credit_terms.html.

28   "Credit card payment calculators," the Calculator Site, accessed August 6, 2018, https://www.thecalculatorsite.com/finance/calculators/credit-card-payment-calculators.php.

29   Promoted by Tim Ferriss.

30   Created by Ramit Sethi, author of *I Will Teach You to Be Rich*.

31   Annie Nova, "Student loan forgiveness gets one-shot, $350M boost," CNBC, accessed August 6, 2018, https://www.cnbc.com/2018/03/26/student-loan-forgiveness-gets-one-shot-350m-boost.html.

32   This specifically applied to federal student loans.

33   Annie Nova, "Student loan nightmare: Some borrowers have to start over," CNBC, accessed August 6, 2018, https://www.cnbc.com/2018/01/12/student-loan-forgiveness-isnt-often-a-forgiving-process.html.

34   "Repayment Assistance Estimator," Government of Canada, accessed August 6, 2018, http://tools.canlearn.ca/cslgs-scpse/cln-cln/rae-ear/rae-ear-1-eng.do.

35   Christine DiGangi, "The Truth About Payday Loans," Credit.com, accessed August 6, 2018, https://www.credit.com/loans/loan-articles/the-truth-about-payday-loans/.

36 Amanda C. Haury, "5 Reasons to Avoid Payday Loans," Investopedia, accessed August 6, 2018, https://www.investopedia.com/financial-edge/0213/5-reasons-to-avoid-payday-loans.aspx.

37 The Pew Charitable Trusts, "Payday lending in America: Who Borrows, Where They Borrow and Why," *Safe Small-Dollar Loans Research Project*, (2012): 11.

38 Car Fox, "Car Depreciation: 5 Things to Consider," Carfax, accessed August 6, 2018, https://www.carfax.com/blog/car-depreciation.

39 "Your Driving Costs: How Much Are You Really Paying to Drive?" AAA Association Communication, accessed August 6, 2018, http://publicaffairsresources.aaa.biz/wp-content/uploads/2014/05/Your-Driving-Costs-2014.pdf.

40 Assuming investing at 9.7% return per year.

41 Robert Digiacomo, "Is Dental Insurance Worth the Cost?" Bankrate, accessed August 6, 2018, https://www.bankrate.com/finance/insurance/dental-insurance-1.aspx.

42 Marilyn Lewis, "Is dental insurance worth the cost?" MoneyWatch, accessed August 6, 2018, https://www.cbsnews.com/news/is-dental-insurance-worth-the-cost/.

43 "WestJet RBC World Elite Mastercard Certificate of Insurance," RBC, accessed August 6, 2018, http://www.rbcroyalbank.com/credit-cards/documentation/pdf/WestJet-World-EliteMasterCard-booklet.pdf.

44 J.D. Roth, "How to Negotiate Your Salary," Lifehacker, accessed August 6, 2018, https://lifehacker.com/how-to-negotiate-your-salary-1566202988.

45 Headhunters, now called recruiters, typically earn a percentage of the salary of the person they place. So, the higher the pay, the more the headhunter receives.

46 Uber surge pricing, at the time of writing, ranges from 1.8x to 2.5x.

47 You may need special insurance to run an Uber or Lyft side business.

48 "How Much Does an Uber Driver Make in 2018?" Ridester, accessed August 6, 2018, https://www.ridester.com/how-much-do-uber-drivers-make/.

49 "Daycare Rates and Passes," Paws Dog Daycare, accessed August 6, 2018, https://www.pawsdogdaycare.ca/dogdaycare/.

50 Jay Baer, "The 13 Critical Podcast Statistics of 2018," ConvinceandConvert, accessed August 6, 2018, http://www.convinceandconvert.com/podcast-research/the-11-critical-podcast-statistics-of-2017/.

51 Diana Kilgour, "Image Consulting Services," Book a Session, accessed August 6, 2018, http://www.dianakilgour.com/session.html.

52 [1] I caution you, however, to clearly specify upfront what the job entails. For example, some clients will ask for endless designs or revisions. Be clear in the scope of the job for fixed-priced gigs.

53 Tim Ferriss, "How to Create a Million-Dollar Business This Weekend," Tim Ferriss Blog, accessed August 6, 2018, https://tim.blog/2011/09/24/how-to-create-a-million-dollar-business-this-weekend-examples-appsumo-mint-chihuahuas/#more-5754.

54 Google "Mint.com original landing page" to see what it looked like initially.

55   "SPDR S&P 500 ETF," State Street Global Advisors, accessed August 7, 2018, https://us.spdrs.com/en/etf/spdr-sp-500-etf-SPY.

56   "iShares Core S&P 500 ETF," iShares by Blackrock, accessed August 7, 2018, https://www.ishares.com/us/products/239726/ishares-core-sp-500-etf.

57   "Vanguard S&P 500 ETF," Vanguard, accessed August 7, 2018, https://investor.vanguard.com/etf/profile/voo.

58   "FTSE Canada All Cap Index ETF (VCN)," Vanguard, accessed August 7, 2018, https://www.vanguardcanada.ca/advisors/adv/en/product.html#/fundDetail/etf/portId=9561/assetCode=equity/?overview.

59   "iShares S&P/TSX 60 Index ETF," Blackrock, accessed August 7, 2018, https://www.blackrock.com/ca/individual/en/products/239832/ishares-sptsx-60-index-etf.

60   "iShares Core S&P/TSX Capped Composite Index ETF," Blackrock, accessed August 7, 2018, https://www.blackrock.com/ca/individual/en/products/239837/ishares-sptsx-capped-composite-index-etf.

61   Back in the day, people would receive a piece of paper called a coupon when they received an interest payment.

62   "Canada Pension Plan- How much you could receive," Canada Pension Plan- Overview, Government of Canada, accessed August 6, 2018, https://www.canada.ca/en/services/benefits/publicpensions/cpp/cpp-benefit/amount.html.

63   "Retirement Plan Access and Participation Across Generations: How Young Workers in the Private Sector Differ From Their Older Colleagues," The Pew Charitable Trusts, accessed August 6, 2018, http://www.pewtrusts.org/en/research-and-analysis/issue-briefs/2017/02/retirement-plan-access-and-participation-across-generations.

64   "The Five-Year Rule for Roth IRA Withdrawals," RothIRA.com, accessed August 6, 2018, https://www.rothira.com/blog/the-five-year-rule-with-roth-ira-withdrawals.

65   "The Pros and Cons of an Early Withdrawal from Your Roth IRA," RothIRA.com, accessed August 6, 2018, https://www.rothira.com/blog/the-pros-and-cons-of-an-early-withdrawal-from-your-roth-ira.

66   Darla Mercado, "New Year, New Tax Brackets. Here's Where You Stand," CNBC, accessed August 6, 2018, https://www.cnbc.com/2017/12/29/heres-where-you-stand-in-the-new-2018-tax-brackets.html.

67   http://www.moneychimp.com/calculator/compound_interest_calculator.htm using a 9.7% interest rate over 20 years

68   "The Five-Year Rule for Roth IRA Withdrawals," RothIRA.com, accessed August 6, 2018, https://www.rothira.com/blog/the-five-year-rule-with-roth-ira-withdrawals.

69   Some examples include tuition, books, supplies, and equipment. Room and board may also be allowed.

70   "RRSP Rules and Regulations," RRSP Basics, RBC, accessed August 6, 2018, http://www.rbcroyalbank.com/products/rrsp/rrsp-rules.html.

71 Suzanne Steel, "Did you over-contribute?" Financial Post, accessed August 6, 2018, http://business.financialpost.com/news/did-you-over-contribute.

72 Jason Heath, "How to know when to start drawing on your RRSP," Financial Post, accessed August 6, 2018, http://business.financialpost.com/personal-finance/retirement/rrsp/how-to-know-when-to-start-drawing-on-your-rrsp.

73 Making RRSP withdrawals before you retire," RRSPs, Get Smarter About Money, accessed August 6, 2018, https://www.getsmarteraboutmoney.ca/plan-manage/retirement-planning/rrsps/making-rrsp-withdrawals-before-you-retire/.

74 "RRSP Rules and Regulations," RRSP Basics, RBC, accessed August 6, 2018, http://www.rbcroyalbank.com/products/rrsp/rrsp-rules.html.

75 "TFSA Withdrawals," RateHub, accessed August 6, 2018, https://www.ratehub.ca/investing/tfsa-withdrawal.

76 "Homeownership rate in selected European countries in 2016," Statista, accessed August 6, 2018, https://www.statista.com/statistics/246355/home-ownership-rate-in-europe/.

77 "Homeownership Rate for the United States," FRED Economic Data, accessed August 6, 2018, https://fred.stlouisfed.org/series/RHORUSQ156N.

78 "Housing in Canada: Key results from the 2016 Census," STATCAN, accessed August 6, 2018, https://www150.statcan.gc.ca/n1/daily-quotidien/171025/dq171025c-eng.htm.

79 Other closing costs, like legal fees, maintenance expenses, or capital gains taxes, ere not included.

80 "What is the return on my real estate investment?" CalcXML, accessed August 6, 2018, https://www.calcxml.com/do/inv04.

81 Brad Case, "Comparing Average REIT Returns and Stocks Over Long Periods, Nareit Market Commentary, Nareit, accessed August 6, 2018, https://www.reit.com/news/blog/market-commentary/comparing-average-reit-returns-and-stocks-over-long-periods.

82 Using the FTSE NAREIT All Equity REITs Index before fees.

83 "S&P 500 Return Calculator, with Dividend Reinvestment," DQYDJ, accessed August 6, 2018, https://dqydj.com/sp-500-return-calculator/.

84 Gavin, "REIT Performance," accessed August 6, 2018, http://www.optionstradingiq.com/reit-performance/.

85 "Vanguard Real Estate ETF," Vanguard, accessed August 6, 2018, https://personal.vanguard.com/us/funds/snapshot?FundIntExt=INT&FundId=0986&funds_disable_redirect=true#tab=1.

86 "Schwab U.S. REIT ETF," Charles Schwab, accessed August 6, 2018, https://www.schwabfunds.com/public/csim/home/products/exchange_traded_funds/performance.html?symbol=SCHH.

87 "iShares U.S. Real Estate ETF," iShares, accessed August 6, 2018, https://www.ishares.com/us/products/239520/ishares-us-real-estate-etf.

88 "iShares S&P/TSX Capped REIT Index ETF," Blackrock, accessed August 6, 2018, https://www.blackrock.com/ca/individual/en/products/239843/ishares-sptsx-capped-reit-index-etf.

89   "BMO Equal Weight REITs Index ETF (ZRE)," Annual Management Report of Fund Performance, BMO, accessed August 6, 2018, https://www.bmo.com/assets/pdfs/gam/etf/a-mrfp/en/A_MRFP_ZRE_E.pdf.

90   FTSE Canadian Capped REIT Index ETF (VRE)," Vanguard, accessed August 6, 2018, https://www.vanguardcanada.ca/individual/indv/en/product.html#/fundDetail/etf/portId=9559/assetCode=equity/?overview.

91   Jussi Askola, "REITs vs. Stocks: Risk Comparison," Seeking Alpha, accessed August 6, 2018, https://seekingalpha.com/article/4061110-reits-vs-stocks-risk-comparison.

92   "What is a debt-to-income ratio? Why is the 43% debt-to-income ratio important?" Consumer Financial Protection Bureau, accessed August 6, 2018, https://www.consumerfinance.gov/ask-cfpb/what-is-a-debt-to-income-ratio-why-is-the-43-debt-to-income-ratio-important-en-1791/.

93   "U.S. Mortgage Calculator with Taxes, Insurance and PMI," FHA Mortgage Calculator, accessed August 6, 2018, https://usmortgagecalculator.org.

94   Andrew Merle, "The Ideal Work Commute Will Make You Happier and Healthier," HuffPost, accessed August 6, 2018, https://www.huffingtonpost.com/entry/the-ideal-work-commute-will-make-you-happier-and-healthier_us_59b-6ca67e4b0bb893fffffd9.

95   Yuqing Pan, "Appreciation Sensation: The Real Factors That Boost Your Home's Bottom Line," Realtor.com, accessed August 6, 2018, https://www.realtor.com/news/trends/which-kinds-of-home-appreciate-fastest/.

96   "Open vs. closed mortgages," LowestRates.ca, accessed August 6, 2018, https://www.lowestrates.ca/mortgage/open-vs-closed.

97   Alyssa Furtado, "What's the Penalty If I Break My Mortgage with Scotiabank?" Ratehub.ca, accessed August 6, 2018, https://www.ratehub.ca/blog/whats-the-penalty-if-i-break-my-mortgage-with-scotiabank/.

98   "How Do Mortgage Prepayment Penalties Work?" ValuePenguin, accessed August 6, 2018, https://www.valuepenguin.com/mortgages/how-mortgage-prepayment-penalties-work.

99   Hal M. Bundrick, "2 Reasons to Get a Home Equity Line of Credit- and a Bunch of Reasons Not to," Nerdwallet.com, accessed August 6, 2018, https://www.nerdwallet.com/blog/mortgages/home-equity-line-credit-heloc-reasons/.

100   JR Hevron, "5 Reasons to Avoid a Home Equity Line of Credit," Mortgageloan.com, accessed August 6, 2018, https://www.mortgageloan.com/5-reasons-avoid-home-equity-line-credit-8685.

101   Gabriel H. Sahlgren, "Work Longer, Live Healthier," *Institute of Economic Affairs*, May page 34.

102   https://www.healthline.com/nutrition/7-health-benefits-of-water#section2